GOLF

Steps to Success

DeDe Owens, EdD
Teaching Professional
Cog Hill Golf & Country Club
Lemont, Illinois

Linda K. Bunker, PhD
Professor, Curry School of Education
University of Virginia, Charlottesville

Leisure Press
Champaign, Illinois

Library of Congress Cataloging-in-Publication Data

Owens, DeDe.
  Golf: steps to success / DeDe Owens, Linda Bunker.
    p. cm.—(Steps to success activity series)
  ISBN 0-88011-321-9
  1. Golf. I. Bunker, Linda K. II. Title. III. Series.
  GV965.O87 1989
  796.352'3—dc19   88-2459

Developmental Editor: Judy Patterson Wright, PhD
Production Director: Ernie Noa
Copy Editor: Peter Nelson
Assistant Editor: Kathy Kane
Proofreader: Laurie McGee
Typesetter: Yvonne Winsor
Text Design: Keith Blomberg
Text Layout: Tara Welsch
Cover Design: Jack Davis
Cover Photo: Bill Morrow
Illustrations By: Raneé Rogers and Gretchen Walters
Printed By: United Graphics, Inc.

Instructional Designer for the Steps to Success Activity Series: Joan N. Vickers, EdD, University of Calgary, Calgary, Alberta, Canada

ISBN: 0-88011-321-9

Printed in the United States of America   10   9

Leisure Press
A Division of Human Kinetics
P.O. Box 5076, Champaign, IL 61825-5076
1-800-747-4457

Canada: Human Kinetics, Box 24040, Windsor, ON N8Y 4Y9
1-800-465-7301 (in Canada only)

Europe: Human Kinetics, P.O. Box IW14, Leeds LS16 6TR, England
0532-781708

Australia: Human Kinetics, P.O. Box 80, Kingswood 5062, South Australia
618-374-0433

New Zealand: Human Kinetics, P.O. Box 105-231, Auckland 1
(09) 309-2259

Contents

Series Preface

The Steps to Success Activity Series is a breakthrough in skill instruction through the development of complete learning progressions—the *steps to success*. These *steps* help students quickly perform basic skills successfully and prepare them to acquire advanced skills readily. At each step, students are encouraged to learn at their own pace and to integrate their new skills into the total action of the activity, which motivates them to achieve.

The unique features of the Steps to Success Activity Series are the result of comprehensive development—through analyzing existing activity books, incorporating the latest research from the sport sciences and consulting with students, instructors, teacher educators, and administrators. This groundwork pointed up the need for three different types of books—for participants, instructors, and teacher educators—which we have created and together comprise the Steps to Success Activity Series.

The *participant book* for each activity is a self-paced, step-by-step guide; learners can use it as a primary resource for a beginning activity class or as a self-instructional guide. The unique features of each *step* in the participant book include

- sequential illustrations that clearly show proper technique for all basic skills,
- helpful suggestions for detecting and correcting errors,
- excellent drill progressions with accompanying *Success Goals* for measuring performance, and
- a complete checklist for each basic skill for a trained observer to rate the learner's technique.

A comprehensive *instructor guide* accompanies the participant's book for each activity, emphasizing how to individualize instruction. Each *step* of the instructor's guide promotes successful teaching and learning with

- teaching cues (*Keys to Success*) that emphasize fluidity, rhythm, and wholeness,
- criterion-referenced rating charts for evaluating a participant's initial skill level,
- suggestions for observing and correcting typical errors,
- tips for group management and safety,
- ideas for adapting every drill to increase or decrease the difficulty level,
- quantitative evaluations for all drills (*Success Goals*), and
- a complete test bank of written questions.

The series textbook, *Instructional Design for Teaching Physical Activities*, explains the *steps to success* model, which is the basis for the Steps to Success Activity Series. Teacher educators can use this text in their professional preparation classes to help future teachers and coaches learn how to design effective physical activity programs in school, recreation, or community teaching and coaching settings.

After identifying the need for participant, instructor, and teacher educator texts, we refined the *steps to success* instructional design model and developed prototypes for the participant and the instructor books. Once these prototypes were fine-tuned, we carefully selected authors for the activities who were not only thoroughly familiar with their sports but had years of experience in teaching them. Each author had to be known as a gifted instructor who understands the teaching of sport so thoroughly that he or she could readily apply the *steps to success* model.

Next, all of the participant and instructor manuscripts were carefully developed to meet the guidelines of the *steps to success* model. Then our production team, along with outstanding artists, created a highly visual, user-friendly series of books.

The result: The Steps to Success Activity Series is the premier sports instructional series available today. The participant books are the best available for helping you to become a master player, the instructor guides will help you to become a master teacher, and the teacher educator's text prepares you to design your own programs.

This series would not have been possible without the contributions of the following:

- Dr. Joan Vickers, instructional design expert,
- Dr. Rainer Martens, Publisher,
- the staff of Human Kinetics Publishers, and
- the *many* students, teachers, coaches, consultants, teacher educators, specialists, and administrators who shared their ideas—and dreams.

Judy Patterson Wright
Series Editor

Preface

Understanding the game of golf is a life-long challenge. The book *Golf: Steps to Success* has provided an opportunity for us as educators to share what we have learned about this game. Our knowledge is based not only on our own past experience and research but also on freely shared information from other teachers and students.

Playing the game of golf requires active participation throughout learning. Within each step (chapter) of this book you will find information about the specific skills required to be successful in golf and strategies for learning these skills. This book differs from other golf books in that it provides clear guidelines for practice and immediate recording of your progress. The sections on error identification and correction provide information that you can use on the practice tee or during a round of golf. Take this book with you when you practice as a handy reference for drills and to review technique. This will allow you an opportunity to have immediate feedback by comparing your performance to the desired goals. All activities are designed to provide a motivating technique for practicing golf, and to help you become a self-learner, for life-long fun and enjoyment.

Just as others have helped us, we hope to help you become a motivated student of golf through this book. We would particularly like to acknowledge the Jemsek family, owners of Cog Hill Golf Course in Lemont Illinois, for the opportunity to constantly challenge and develop our teaching philosophy. Like most knowledge, ours has come from many sources, including fellow golf professionals and educators. Though it would be impossible to acknowledge each one individually, we would like to thank them collectively for the years of sharing ideas about the game of golf and the challenges of teaching it.

DeDe Owens
Linda K. Bunker

The Steps to Success Staircase

Get ready to climb a staircase—one that will lead you to become a great golfer. You cannot leap to the top; you get there by climbing one step at a time.

Each of the 16 steps you will take is an easy transition from the one before. The first few steps of the staircase provide a foundation—a solid foundation of basic skills and concepts. As you progress further, you will be able to execute the basic golf swing and modify it to meet any situation on the golf course. You will learn to choose the proper clubs and swing to match your various golf needs—whether for loft, trajectory, or distance. As you near the top of the staircase, the climb eases, and you'll find that you have developed a sense of confidence in your golf ability that makes further progress a real joy.

Familiarize yourself with this section as well as the sections ''Equipment,'' and ''Preparing Your Body for Success'' for an orientation and in order to understand how to set up your practice sessions around the steps.

Follow the same sequence each step (chapter) of the way:

1. Read the explanations of what is covered in the step, why the step is important, and how to execute or perform the step's focus, which may be a basic skill, concept, tactic, or combination of them.

2. Follow the numbered illustrations showing exactly how to position your body to execute each basic skill successfully. There are three general parts to each skill: preparation (getting into a starting position), execution (performing the skill that is the focus of the step), and follow-through (recovering to starting position).

3. Look over the common errors that may occur and the recommendation of how to correct them.

4. The drills help you improve your skills through repetition and purposeful practice. Read the directions and the Success Goal for each drill. Practice accordingly and record your score. Compare your score with the Success Goal for the drill. You need to meet the Success Goal of each drill before moving on to practice the next one, because the drills are arranged in an easy-to-difficult progression. This sequence is designed specifically to help you achieve continual success.

5. As soon as you can reach all the Success Goals for one step, you are ready for a qualified observer—such as your teacher, coach, or trained partner—to evaluate your basic skill technique against the Keys to Success Checklist. This is a qualitative, or subjective, evaluation of your technique or form—because using correct form enhances your performance. Your evaluator can tailor specific goals for you, if needed, by using the blank Individual Program sheet (Appendix A) and the Shotkeeper Scorecard (Appendix B).

6. Repeat these procedures for each of the 16 Steps to Success. Then rate yourself according to the directions for ''Rating Your Golf Progress.''

Good luck on your step-by-step journey of developing your golf skills, building confidence, experiencing success—and having fun on the way!

The Game of Golf

The exact origin of golf is unknown. Some historians believe the earliest form of golf may have emerged in Greece, where ancient shepherds hit stones with their staffs. However, the game as we know it today had its origins in St. Andrews, Scotland, around 1744. In 1888 the first officially recorded golf club was established in Yonkers, New York, by three Scotsmen. This first course had 6 holes scattered through cow pastures and apple groves and was named in honor of their Scottish homeland course, St. Andrews. Today a regulation course has 18 holes and may cover as many as 250 acres of beautifully groomed countryside. Golf is enjoyed today as a popular recreational activity. It can lead to various levels of competition. Golf is also a growing spectator sport, professional and amateur tournaments becoming very popular.

PLAYING A GAME

The object of the game of golf is to hit a small, hard ball—the *golf ball*—as few times as is necessary for it to travel from its starting point, a *tee*, into the *hole* located on each green. The golf ball is struck with clubs designated as *woods* or *irons*. Each player must hit his or her own stationary ball in the desired direction and for the desired distance, using one of a variety of clubs of assorted lengths and shapes. Each attempt to strike the ball, whether successful or unsuccessful, is called a *stroke*. Your score for a hole is the total number of strokes it takes you to hit the ball from the tee into the hole.

You may play a game of golf alone or in a group with one to three other players. Golf is played on golf courses with 9 or 18 holes. The holes vary in length from 85 to 600 yards and are generally referred to as short holes (85–245 yards), medium holes (245–445 yards) or long holes (445–600 yards). The total yardage of a regulation 18-hole golf course varies from 5,600 to 7,200 yards.

In addition to the lengths of the holes, golf courses have other characteristics that provide challenges to players (see Figure 1). Each hole begins with a *tee box* from which the first ball must be hit. Each hole ends on a *green*, which has a 4 1/4-inch diameter hole, or *cup*, cut down into the earth. Between the tee and the green is the *fairway*. The course is designed with specific boundaries that are marked by out-of-bounds stakes. A player who hits a ball outside the boundary or into water is penalized by having one stroke added to the score.

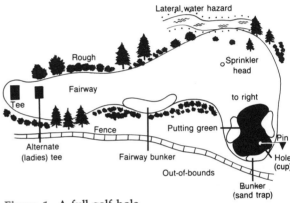

Figure 1 A full golf hole.

All golf holes have the five components described: teeing area, fairway, rough, putting green, and cup (hole). The central path from tee to green is the fairway, and it is the preferred location for your ball's landing. These areas may be wide or narrow, smooth or rough, and may have trees and shrubs located within them. Unfortunately, sometimes shots land in the taller grass left alongside the fairway, called the *rough*, which may also have natural obstacles such as trees and wooded areas. The ball may also land in sand or water hazards. Such challenges on the golf course are called *hazards* or *trouble*.

SCORING

Your ability as a golfer is measured by the number of strokes it takes you to complete each hole. The count begins with the first attempt to hit the ball off the tee. One stroke is counted each time you attempt to hit the ball (whether it is contacted or not) until it goes into the cup on the green of that hole. Your score for a round of golf is the total number of strokes for the 9 or 18 holes played. Lower scores are indicative of better players and are normally reported as the total of 18 holes, which is called a *round*.

It is possible to compete against another golfer and win by using fewer strokes to complete the round. Otherwise, you may wish to measure your ability against a designated standard of excellence called *par*. Par is the number of strokes judged to be necessary for a very good golfer to complete a hole. It is assumed that a golfer requires two putts once the ball has landed on the green. If you add to the putts the number of shots it should take to reach the green, you can determine par. The number of strokes is determined by the length of the hole: par 3s are short holes (85–245 yards), requiring only one stroke from tee to green and two putts; par 4s are medium-length holes (245–445 yards); and par 5s are long holes (over 445 yards). If you are a very good golfer and you play a 480-yard hole, for example, it should take you three shots to get to the green and two putts, for a par 5. In order to add challenge to a golf course, the lengths of holes are varied. On a typical 18-hole course, there are four par 3s, ten par 4s, and four par 5s, for a course par of 72.

There are terms in golf that reflect how you score on a hole relative to par. An *ace* is a hole on which it took only one swing to land in the hole, otherwise known as a *hole-in-one*. This is a very unusual occasion and is cause for great celebration! An *eagle* refers to 2 strokes under par on a hole, whereas a *birdie* is 1 stroke under par. It is common to take more strokes than par; taking 1 stroke more than par is called a *bogey*, whereas 2 strokes over par is referred to as a *double bogey*.

BASIC RULES

The rules of golf are designed to provide a fair chance for all players to play at their best levels and to compete fairly against one another or against the course (against par). The rules provide the framework for direction and order in the game, so the sooner you understand them, the more fun you will have. If you do not use them as intended, you may find yourself need-lessly penalized or accused of playing unfairly or cheating.

Golf rules are often described by the nature of the penalties incurred for certain course conditions or behaviors. When a rule is violated, it can result in penalties of 1 or 2 strokes, or disqualification. There are also some conditions on the course over which you have no control and for which you are therefore not assessed a penalty.

The official rules of golf contain specifications related to the actions of players preparing to strike the ball, conditions surrounding the ball at rest, and course conditions independent of the player's control. A brief review of the most important rules for stroke play (which is more often used by beginners than in match play) and commonly encountered situations are now presented here. However, when you are truly ready to compete, you should purchase an official rule book and read the rules of golf published by the United States Golf Association, Far Hills, NJ, 07931.

No Penalty: Free Drop

Shots coming to rest in the conditions listed here are beyond your control and therefore do not result in penalties. If you find yourself in any of these situations, you may hit the ball as it lies. Otherwise, "seek relief" with a *free drop*, which allows you to relocate the ball in the fairest way possible. To *drop* a ball at the *nearest point of relief* means to stand outside the trouble area, face the hole, extend your arm at shoulder height, and literally drop the ball (see Figure 2). The ball must be dropped

staked tree

Figure 2 Golfer "dropping" a ball to seek relief.

within one club length of the point of release and come to rest at a spot no nearer the hole than the original spot from which relief was sought.

1. *Ground under repair*, marked with a sign or white paint

2. *Staked trees* or shrubs

3. *Sprinkler heads* for course watering (see Figure 3)

4. *Casual water* from rain or sprinklers (see Figure 4)

5. *Holes* made by burrowing animals

Figure 3 A sprinkler head.

Figure 4 Casual water.

One-Stroke Penalty

Each of the following situations results in a one-stroke penalty. In addition, there are specific procedures required in order to continue. These specifications are provided with each of the following situations.

1. A *lost ball* is one that cannot be found within 5 minutes. "Drop" another ball at the point from which original ball was hit, or retee if originally hit from the teeing area (see Figure 5).

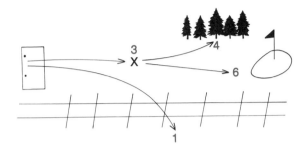

Figure 5 Assume first ball went out-of-bounds. Return to tee and hit (penalty + stroke = 3). Land at X. Hit ball out-of-bounds into woods, return to X and hit (penalty + stroke = 6).

2. An *out-of-bounds* ball is one that has gone beyond the white stakes placed on the perimeter of the golf course. (If any part of the ball lies inbounds, the ball is considered inbounds and in play.) Go back to the spot from which the ball was hit and drop it, or retee a ball hit from the teeing area.

3. A *direct water hazard* is water that runs across the fairway, perpendicular to the fairway. It is usually marked by yellow stakes that designate that the hazard consists of all the area within the stakes, which may include marshy ground and other land, as well as water (see Figure 6).

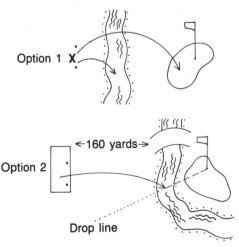

Figure 6 Direct water hazard.

Option 1:

Go back to original spot (X) and drop another ball.

Option 2:

Keeping on line with the point where the ball crossed the margin of the hazard, go back away from the pin as far as desired and drop the ball.

4. A *lateral water hazard* is water that runs parallel to the fairway. It is usually marked with red stakes designating that every point within that area is considered part of the hazard (see Figure 7).

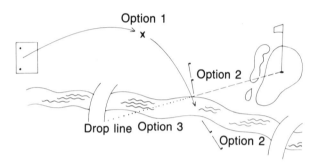

Figure 7 Lateral water hazard.

Option 1:

Go back to the shot's original spot and drop another ball.

Option 2:

Determine where the ball would have crossed the far margin of the hazard had it gone over it. Drop a ball within 2 club lengths of that spot, but no closer to the hole.

Option 3:

Go to the far side of the hazard directly across from where the ball entered the hazard. Drop a ball as far away as desired on the line that could be drawn from the pin through the ball.

5. An *unplayable lie* is any shot you consider unplayable. It can be any ball except one in a water hazard (see Figure 8).

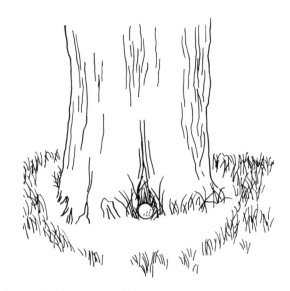

Figure 8 An unplayable lie.

Option 1:

Go back to original spot and drop another ball.

Option 2:

Drop a ball within 2 club lengths of the ball's position, but no closer to the hole.

Option 3:

Go back as far as desired to drop the ball on a line from the pin through the unplayable point.

6. An *accidental moving of ball* occurs when a ball moves from its original position because a player accidentally touches it. Ball must be returned to its original position.

7. *Whiffing* is an attempt to hit the ball in which no contact is made. This is the same as a strike in baseball. The swing counts as a stroke; leave the ball there and try again!

Two-Stroke Penalty

Each of the following situations results in a 2-stroke penalty, and must be accompanied by the following actions if specified.

1. *Grounding the Club in a Hazard.* You must not let your club touch the ground while in a hazard, whether preparing to

strike the ball or on the backswing. The club may touch the hazard as part of the forwardswing, though (see Figure 9).

Figure 9 Grounding a club in a hazard (at any time before the actual swing).

2. *Hitting the Wrong Ball.* If you discover you have hit the wrong ball, find the correct ball and play it. Count only the strokes taken on the correct ball, but add a 2-stroke penalty.

3. *Hitting a Ball or Flag on the Green.* When putting from the green, you must not hit the flag or another golfer's ball. It is your responsibility to have the flag tended and moved aside (see Figure 10). Also, it's up to you to have an opponent ''mark'' his or her ball if it is in the way of your putt. Play the ball from where it comes to rest. An opponent's ball that has been moved must be replaced to its original position.

4. *Requesting Assistance.* In regulation play, only general course knowledge may be requested from others. For example, you may ask for the length of a hole, but it is not legal to ask for advice about what club to use or to request help on your swing.

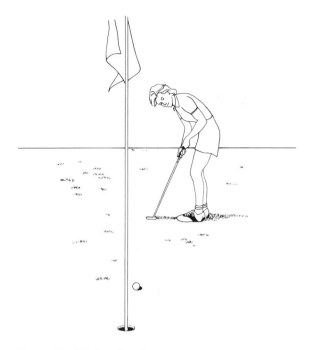

Figure 10 Hitting flag from green.

Disqualification

1. You can be disqualified for hitting the wrong ball and not correcting the error prior to teeing off on the next hole. To avoid this, check the ball before you swing to be sure that it is yours.

2. You can be disqualified for making an error in scoring, assigning a lower score than you earned to any hole.

Some of the rules of golf require that you return to the place of an original shot after assessing a penalty. If you have hit a long drive, this can be a problem in that it takes a great deal of time to go down to look for the ball and then walk all the way back to the original spot to hit another ball. For this reason, it may be a good idea to hit a *provisional ball*. A provisional ball is a ball played from the same spot as the last shot, when it is feared that the original ball has just landed out-of-bounds or lost outside a water hazard. If the original ball is found inbounds, it must be played; the provisional ball must then not be used.

The rules of golf are not always easy to interpret or remember. It is therefore a good idea to carry a rule book in your golf bag. If you are playing in a tournament and are in doubt as to the interpretation of a rule, ask for assistance from tournament officials. It is also sometimes appropriate to agree among playing partners to reinterpret strict rules during the learning stages or if playing conditions are very poor. For example, in early spring some golf courses allow you to improve your ball's lie, due to the large number of bare spots on the courses. This is sometimes referred to as playing *winter rules*.

Sometimes rules are so difficult to interpret that there is a question of what to do. In that case, it is possible to play a second, or *alternate ball* for the rest of a hole. The player must state which ball will count after a ruling is obtained. If it is not stated prior to playing the two balls, the ball with the higher score must count.

As a player, you are responsible for knowing the rules and playing by them. Unfortunately, not all players know the rules, and/or some choose not to apply them. If you are playing with such a player, consider your options: inform him or her of the rules, share your rule book, assess the penalty, or ignore him or her and play your own game. In a tournament, you must inform this golfer of the rule. If the infraction is not corrected, assess the penalty. In social golf, the decision is up to you.

GOLF ETIQUETTE

There are many unwritten courtesy rules that are an integral part of the game of golf. For example, only one golfer ever hits at any one time. Though there is no penalty for violating a "rule" of etiquette, such offenses are considered extremely rude and unacceptable. By the way, in this example, the order of taking turns should generally be determined by which golfer has farther to go to get to the hole.

Etiquette is very important in golf. Because there are several important concepts related to etiquette, an entire step on etiquette has been included in this book (see Step 13).

GOLF TODAY

Golf is truly a lifetime sport for people of all ages and abilities. The handicapping system makes golf an ideal sport in which players of differing abilities can compare their performances or compete against each other. Your golf *handicap* is an equalizer that you can subtract from your score. For example, if your home course has a course rating (established by the USGA) of 72.4 and you score 100, the difference is 28 strokes. If you regularly shoot 100 (and have submitted at least ten scores to your golf pro at the course), you would be assigned a handicap of 27 (calculated as 96% of the difference between your average score and the course rating for that course). If you have questions about determining your handicap, talk with the professional at your home course or your golf instructor.

This pre-sloping handicapping system (see page 9) is designed and monitored by the USGA, the governing body of golf in the United States. The USGA also provides the official rules of golf and reviews new developments in equipment and the structure of golf balls in order to keep the game fair.

When you are ready to test your skills in competition you will find many opportunities. Public golf courses often sponsor tournaments for players of all levels. In some tournaments the score that counts is your *gross score*, or the total of all the strokes you take. In other tournaments you are allowed to subtract your handicap from your gross score for a *net score*. However in *open tournaments*, where professionals and amateurs all can participate, your gross score is the only one used.

There are several organizations that provide clinics and lessons for golfers. Most public and private golf clubs have golf professionals who belong to either the Ladies Professional Golf Association (LPGA) or the Professional Golfers' Association (PGA, with both men and women professionals). Be sure to look for a qualified professional; check with others who have taken lessons with this pro before you invest in a series of lessons.

If you wish to read more about the game or need additional information, contact the National Golf Foundation (NGF). This is a nonprofit organization that provides clinics for teachers, assistance to golf courses, and educational materials on the game of golf. There are also school golf programs sponsored by NGF and the American Alliance for Health, Physical Education, Recreation, and Dance (AAHPERD). Many private organizations, such as Golf Digest, offer clinics and schools for private individuals or clubs.

You will never be too good to quit learning about the game of golf. From the beginner to professional, most golfers are students of the game all their lives. Half the fun is learning how to hit a draw or hook when you want to—and not when it happens to you. You can learn to challenge a course in the same way that you accept challenges and opportunities in other aspects of your life, for golf is a lifetime sport.

Drills on the Game of Golf

1. Test Your Terminology

Understanding and using the proper terminology is important in communicating with other players and in enjoying the game of golf. Practice your terminology by naming and defining the parts of a golf hole and by identifying the terms for scoring. Check your answers with the preceding section and Figure 1.

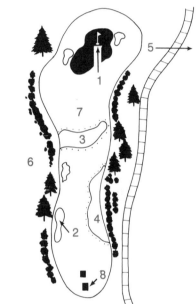

Figure 11 Parts of a golf hole.

Success Goal =
a. correctly label the parts of the golf hole diagrammed in Figure 11 (above)
b. match the terms with their definitions

Your Score =

a. 1. _____
   2. _____
   3. _____
   4. _____
   5. _____
   6. _____
   7. _____
   8. _____

b. match the terms with their definitions

Term	Definition
birdie _____	1. a hole-in-one
bogey _____	2. two over par
ace _____	3. two under par
double bogey _____	4. one under par
eagle _____	5. one over par

2. Practice at Scoring

All golfers should know the basic rules of golf. Each player is responsible for his or her own actions during play. The following situations requiring rulings are typical of those found on the course. Respond to each question; then check your answers by rereading the section on rules.

Lost Ball. You have hit your third shot into the woods and cannot find your ball.

Success Goal = answer each of the following questions correctly

    a. Where do you play your next shot?

    b. What is the penalty?

    c. How many strokes will you have after you play your next ball?

Your Score = (#) _____ correct answers

    a. _____

    b. _____

    c. _____

Ball in a Hazard. You have hit your tee shot into a lateral water hazard.

Success Goal = answer each of the following questions correctly

    a. What options do you have for playing your next shot?

    b. What is the penalty?

    c. How many strokes will you have after you play your next shot?

Your Score = (#) _____ correct answers

    a. _____

    b. _____

    c. _____

Out-of-Bounds. You have hit your fourth stroke out-of-bounds.

Success Goal = answer each of the following questions correctly

    a. Where do you play your next shot?

    b. What is the penalty?

    c. How many strokes will you have after you play your next shot?

Your Score = (#) _____ correct answers

    a. _____

    b. _____

    c. _____

Whiff. You have made 2 swing attempts to hit your tee shot. On the third attempt, you hit the ball about 50 yards into the fairway.

Success Goal = answer each of the following questions correctly

    a. Where do you play your next shot?

    b. What is the penalty?

    c. How many strokes will you have after you play your next shot?

Your Score = (#) _____ correct answers

    a. _____

    b. _____

    c. _____

Casual Water. You are playing after a heavy rainstorm, and your ball lands in a water puddle.

Success Goal = answer each of the following questions correctly

    a. Where do you play your next shot?

    b. What is the penalty?

    c. How many strokes will you have after you play your next shot?

Your Score = (#) _____ correct answers

    a. _____

    b. _____

    c. _____

3. Determining Your Handicap*

The handicapping system in golf is an advantage to all golfers because it allows golfers of all ability levels to compete together on more equal terms. Determine your handicap, supposing you shot 10 rounds of golf with the following scores: 120, 100, 98, 105, 97, 100, 94, 95, 98, and 97. The course rating is 72.6. Round your figures to the nearest whole number.

    If possible, actually play 10 rounds of golf and determine your own handicap. If you play only 9 holes at a time, not 18, simply double the score for each round. After you have once determined your handicap, update it by always using the 10 best rounds out of the last 20 rounds you played.

Success Goals = determine handicaps (a) for the imagined scores given, and (b) for your actual scores after playing 10 rounds of golf; then check your method of calculation by referring to the description of the pre-sloping handicapping system within the "Golf Today" section

Your Score =

a. _____ handicap with imaginary scores [answer = 27]

b. _____ your own real handicap

---

*This drill uses the USGA pre-sloping system for calculating handicaps, which is an appropriate estimate for beginning golfers. Effective March 1, 1991, the official USGA handicapping system is the sloping system, which is more appropriate for competition.

The game of golf is played with a set of golf clubs and a small, hard ball. Most golfers use a set of 14 clubs, which are in a golf bag. As you get better, or now if you prefer, you may wish to have golf shoes and a golf glove to give you a better grip on your club.

GOLF CLUBS

A set of golf clubs is generally composed of 14 clubs: nine irons, four woods, and a putter (see Figure 12). The irons generally range from a 3-iron to a 9-iron, a pitching wedge (PW) and a sand wedge (SW). The woods range from a 1-wood, or driver, to a 7-wood.

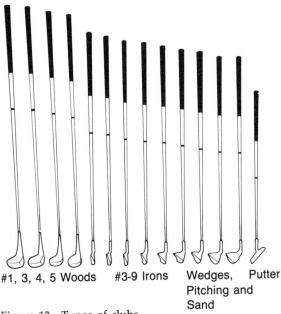

#1, 3, 4, 5 Woods   #3-9 Irons   Wedges, Pitching and Sand   Putter

Figure 12 Types of clubs.

Irons and woods vary in club shaft length and the loft (backward slant) of the clubface, which determine shot distance and trajectory. As the numbers increase, the loft increases and the shaft length decreases, making for higher trajectories over shorter distances. The lower the number and the longer the shaft, the greater the potential distance and the flatter, or lower, the trajectory.

Initially a beginner's set might include a 7-wood, 3-iron, 5-iron, 7-iron, 9-iron, PW, SW,

and putter. Clubs can often be rented or purchased at golf courses. Clubs can be purchased from club professionals, discount centers, sporting good shops, and department stores in a variety of styles (and for a variety of prices). The choice of club brand depends on the aesthetic appeal of the club to you, the characteristics of the club's actions, and what is available within your price range. Be sure to consult your instructor, local golf professional, or dealer for assistance.

Your major concern in obtaining clubs should be that they are appropriate for your height, hand size, and strength. Clubs come in assorted sizes and should be fit to you—not you to them. Clubs that are either too short or too long, are too light or too heavy, or have grips that are too small or too large can inhibit your ability to learn the game effectively, no matter what your ability or interest.

It is important that you know your clubs and can refer to them with the appropriate names and terms for the various parts. Figure 13 illustrates the parts of the club.

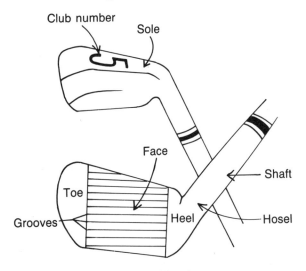

Figure 13 Parts of a clubhead.

Woods

Two types of woods are on the market today: the traditional and the metal. Traditional woods are solid hardwood (e.g., persimmon), or made of wood laminates that are much cheaper and probably equally effective for most golfers. Both types of woods are numbered 1 through 7.

Metal woods have become popular since the late 1970s and have been nicknamed *Pittsburgh Persimmon*. When compared with traditional woods, metal woods have an advantage in producing speed and control. The harder surface from which the ball rebounds and the more equal weight distribution provide for more consistency. The smaller hosel design reduces wind resistance, thereby increasing clubhead speed with the same swing force.

Irons

There are two basic iron constructions: the traditional forged iron and the more recent cast iron. The forged iron is less expensive to produce and performs about the same as the cast iron. The choice is merely up to personal preference.

There are some differences between irons and the way they look and perform (see Figure 14). For example, some clubs have a very good

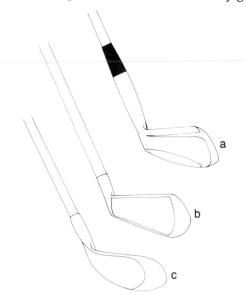

Figure 14 Club designs for irons: (a) traditional, (b) heel-toe weight distribution, (c) sole weighting.

balance between the heel and toe, whereas others are lighter the farther away from the center of the blade. There are also low-profile irons, which are heavier in the *sole*, or bottom,

to help get the ball airborne and travel at a higher trajectory. Some irons also have a wider, flatter sole, which reduces its normal digging effect. Irons are numbered 1 through 9 and also include the sand wedge and the pitching wedge.

LENGTHS OF CLUBS

Golf clubs come in two standard lengths and many variations in between. However, the size of club that is perfect for you depends upon many different factors, including your height, length of arms, preferred posture when hitting a ball, and club loft. Because of these complex variables, you should seek the help of your teacher or pro to determine which clubs are best for you at this stage.

GRIPS

Because your hands are the only thing that directly control the club, it is important that the grip on your club is appropriate for you. Grips are made with a variety of materials and textures—leather, rubber, smooth, rough. The type of grip you choose is solely your personal preference, so try several different types.

Your grip should fit your hand size (see Figure 15). Hold the club by the grip; the recommended fit is one in which the middle finger of your target (upper) hand just touches the palm. If your grip is too large or too small, it affects your hand action and your ability to control the club.

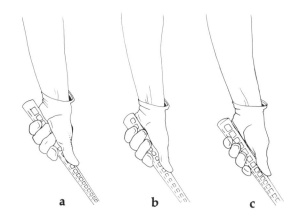

Figure 15 (a) Too small—palm of hand overlaps fingers; (b) proper fit—index finger of target hand touches the palm; (c) too large—space between the fingers and the palm.

OTHER CHARACTERISTICS OF GOLF CLUBS

Golf clubs come with different amounts of flexibility in their shafts, and with different overall weights. In general, you should seek the aid of a golf professional or teacher to assist in fitting your clubs to you.

Many different shafts are available today, and are made of a variety of metals, alloys, and other materials (e.g., graphite, titanium, steel, fiberglass) with different weights and amounts of flexibility. *Flexibility* refers to the amount of bending in the shaft and is rated by letters (A, B, C, D), by numbers (1, 2, 3, 4), or simply by words (from very flexible to extra stiff). The degree of flexibility affects your ability to control the club. Imagine trying to swing a club whose shaft is as flexible as a garden hose or jump rope; this wouldn't give you much of a shot.

The shaft flexibility you need depends on your strength and swing speed. Generally, a golfer who is stronger or has faster swings can accommodate a stiffer shaft. The majority of players' needs fall within the "regular" range of shaft flexibility.

Golf clubs also vary in swing weight, or overall weight. *Swing weight* refers to the club's weight distribution from the grip to the head. Most clubs are rated from C to D though the range is from A to E. A club with an overall weight that is too light or too heavy is difficult to control during the swing, and this affects shot distance and accuracy.

GOLF BALLS

Golf balls come in a variety of types from the most popular solid construction to a wound ball. The solid construction is more durable and has a distance edge. The solid ball is therefore recommended for most beginning and intermediate golfers. The type of ball construction is not indicated on the ball itself, but often on the packages in which it is sold. If you are in doubt, be sure to ask.

GOLF SHOES

Golf shoes are recommended as you begin to practice and play. They provide better traction, which helps you in learning good footwork and weight transfer. Golf shoes are also important as you walk the course and practice for extended periods of time because of the better support provided as compared to tennis shoes. However, tennis shoes are fine initially, especially those that give you good lateral (side) support.

GOLF GLOVES

A golf glove is beneficial if your hands tend to perspire or if your hands are soft or easily irritated. A golf glove is generally worn on the target-side hand and can be made of any of a variety of styles and fabrics. Whether you wear a golf glove is a matter of personal preference.

Preparing Your Body for Success

A warm-up period is needed in golf, as in other sports. However, the major emphasis for a golf warm-up is not on increasing your heart rate, but on increasing flexibility and strength. The turning and twisting motion of the golf swing utilizes muscles in various combinations that are not normally exercised in everyday activities. Prior to practicing and playing, 5–10 minutes should be spent warming up, doing flexibility exercises to stretch the muscles used during the swing motion. These exercises help you improve your swing and prevent injuries.

WHY IS IT IMPORTANT TO PREPARE YOUR BODY FOR SUCCESS THROUGH PROPER WARM-UP?

Allowing your body to warm up before practicing or playing a round of golf is important in order to ensure a safe and enjoyable experience. It is also important to be sure that your body can move in the ways necessary to be a successful golfer. Golf requires your body to stretch and move through a wide range of motion.

HOW TO PREPARE YOUR BODY FOR SUCCESS: WARMING-UP

Because golf is a self-paced activity, cardiovascular endurance is not as important as in some other sports. However, when playing a long round of golf, your physical stamina is important. You must have adequate muscular endurance to play for 4–5 hours in a row and to walk the entire distance of the 18 holes (well over 4 miles). See Figure 16 for a summary of how to warm-up properly. The first phase in preparing your body for success is therefore to get your blood circulating in order to help your muscles stretch. Select and complete one warm-up exercise from Phase I. Then select one exercise per body part listed under the flexibility exercises in Phase II. You will get a head-to-toe warm-up and be ready to practice and play at an optimal level.

Figure 16 Keys to Success: *The Warm-Up*

Preparation Phase

1. Get your blood moving
2. Increase circulation through aerobic exercises

Flexibility Phase

Work from head to toes
a. head
b. neck
c. shoulders
d. lower back
e. legs
f. arms and hands

EXERCISES TO PREPARE YOUR BODY FOR SUCCESS

Each day you should complete a two-phase warm-up. The first phase involves aerobic exercise such as jumping rope to get your heart pumping and your blood moving faster. The second phase should involve a systematic program of flexibility exercises to stretch the muscles in all of your body parts.

Phase I: Exercises to Get Your Blood Moving

It is important to allow your body to warm up before you practice or play. Complete one of the following exercises before each practice session and before you play a round of golf.

1. Jogging in place for 3 minutes
2. Jumping rope for 100 counts
3. Taking a brisk, 5-minute walk while carrying your golf bag

Phase II: Flexibility Exercises

Concentrate on how your body feels as you perform the following exercises. A properly stretched muscle resists injury and allows your body to turn more during your golf swing. This increased range of motion can increase the distance you can hit a golf ball.

Start from your head and work down so that you are sure to stretch each body part. Select one exercise for each body part. Also, at the end of your practice period or round of golf, be sure to take advantage of a cool-down period. If you have been working hard, your body should be warmer and more flexible than it was at the beginning. Use this time to repeat at least one exercise for each of the body parts identified.

2. Standing, relax your head downward and gradually lift your chin to the right, making a complete circle around to the back, to the left, and around to your starting point. Then reverse the direction. Repeat in each direction 6 times.

Head and Neck

1. Standing, turn your head to the right side. With your left hand, gently push back against your jaw as if to have your chin touch your right shoulder. Hold the stretch for a count of 15. Turn your head to the left using the same procedure. Repeat in each direction 6 times.

Shoulders

1. Standing, extend your right arm at shoulder height across your chest toward your left shoulder. Place your left hand on your right elbow. Gently bring your right arm closer to your chest by applying gentle pulling pressure with your left hand. Hold this position for 10 seconds. Then reverse the direction by bringing your left arm across

your body at shoulder height and applying gentle pressure with your right hand. Repeat in each direction 6 times.

2. Standing, raise your arms to the side to shoulder height. Begin to make small circular movements with your arms. Increase the size of the circles until they are as large as possible. Then gradually begin to reduce the size of the circles. Repeat 10 times, resting briefly between sessions and alternating the direction of the circles. (Note: This exercise helps with both strength and flexibility.)

Lower Back

1. Standing, place a club behind your neck and across your shoulders, holding the club with a hand at each end. Without moving

your hips, turn your shoulders to the right. Hold the stretch for a count of 15. Reverse and turn to left. Repeat each direction 6 times.

2. Sit on the floor with your legs extended in front. Bend your right leg at the knee and place your right foot on the floor on the outside of the left knee. Hold a club across the front of your shoulders, under your chin. Turn your trunk to the left as far as possible. Hold the stretch for 10 seconds. Repeat 6 times. To repeat to the right side, switch so your left leg crosses over the right and your body turns to the right.

3. Standing with your arms extended overhead, hold a club at the center of its shaft with both hands. Bend your upper body to the left and hold for 10 seconds. Then bend to the right and hold. Repeat to both sides 6 times.

Legs

1. Standing with your feet together, hold a club with a hand at each end. Cross your right foot over the left. Slowly bend over, allowing your upper body to relax as your arms hang down toward the ground. The club should hang as close to the ground as possible. Hold for 10 seconds. Repeat 6 times. Then switch so your left foot crosses over your right foot. Hang and hold. Repeat 6 times on this side, too.

2. Sitting on the floor with your legs out straight and toes pointed, hold a club in your hands. Lean your chest out over your knees as far as possible. Reach gently toward your ankles, holding the stretch for 15 seconds. Do not bounce. Repeat 6 times, returning to the relaxed position between each repetition.

Arms and Hands

1. Hold a golf club in the center of its shaft with one hand, your arm at your side. Bend your arm at the elbow and extend your forearm horizontally, holding your elbow close to your body. Rotate your forearm, causing the club to turn clockwise; then repeat counterclockwise. The club should make a half circle as it turns around your arm as its axis. Repeat the rotation 10 times and then switch to the opposite hand. Exercise each arm 6 times. (Note: This exercise is good for both strength and flexibility.)

2. Standing, hold a golf club in the center of its shaft with one hand, your arm at your side. Bend your arm at the elbow and extend the forearm horizontally, the elbow

tucked close to your body. Hold the club vertically so that its ends point toward the sky and earth. Move the club so that your thumb comes closer to your forearm, points to your shoulder, then points away from your shoulder.

Step 1 Experiencing the Full Swing Motion

Your first basic golf skill to learn is the full swing motion. The full swing motion is the foundation for the golf swing. In this step you learn to control your body in its largest swinging motion by practicing without a club and ball (which will be added in Steps 2 and 3). Once you have learned the full swing motion, it will be easy to alter its motion and length to produce the variety of other swings needed in golf. By learning the full swing first, you will also be able to detect slight variations in your body posture and tension in executing any golf swing.

WHY IS THE FULL SWING MOTION IMPORTANT?

The full swing is used on all shots from the teeing area, the starting point for each hole, through shots near the green. It is used with all of the woods and irons, unless the full swing motion with the 9-iron would cause the ball to go too far. The full swing is often called the *distance swing*. During a round of golf, you use the full swing for about 50% of the strokes. The other 50% are divided between strokes requiring less than a full swing and putting.

HOW TO EXECUTE THE FULL SWING

The key to developing a good golf swing is to understand that it is basically a simple swinging motion. Imagine the motion of a pendulum or a swing in the park (see Figure 1.1). The motion is continuous and creates an arc around a center. The center for your golf swing is your sternum, or breastbone.

An important concept to remember as you begin to learn the golf swing is that the ball merely gets in the way of the swinging motion. In golf, the ball is stationary; thus, the primary objective is developing a single consistent, repeatable swing. In sports such as tennis, volleyball, and racquetball, the objective is to hit a moving ball, which requires developing swing adaptations to adjust for the speed and direction of the moving ball.

Figure 1.1 The golf swing as a pendulum.

When the golf swing is described, it is common to use terms that refer to the target and the phases of the swing. The target is ultimately the hole with a *flag*, sometimes called a *pin*, inserted in it. When referring to the target, this book uses the phrases *target side* and *rear side*. When you hit a golf ball, you are standing sideways to the target. If you are right-handed, your left side is closest to the hole and is called your *target side*, whereas your right arm and leg are on the *rear side*. If you are left-handed, these terms are reversed: Your target side is the right side of your body, and your rear side is your left side. Using the terms *target side* and *rear side* allows you to use this book equally well whether you're a right- or left-handed golfer. Finally, rather than always using the word *side* in differentiating between body parts, this book sometimes simply uses *target* and *rear*, as in ''target knee'' (short for ''target-side knee'') and ''rear foot.''

The golf swing has three phases: preparation, execution, and follow-through. The *preparation phase* or preswing setup position, is the ready position from which you begin to swing (see Figure 1.2). To take your setup position, pick an imaginary target and place a club on the ground pointing to this target. The line from club to target is called the *target line*. In your mind draw a line parallel to the target line, with about 2 1/2 feet between the two lines. Stand with your toes on this parallel line, your feet shoulder width apart. This is called a *square stance*. Bend forward from the top of your thighs at an angle of about 45 degrees, keeping your back straight. Let your arms hang relaxed from your shoulders. Maintaining this position, flex your knees slightly. Feel your weight distributed evenly between both feet. You should center your weight between the midstep and the balls of your feet in such a way that you can more easily tap your heels than your toes.

Figure 1.2 Arm swing setup with club as target line.

The *execution phase* is the actual swinging motion, consisting of the backswing and forwardswing. The *backswing* is the motion that swings your arms and club back from the ball and to the rear. You start the backswing by swinging your arms, hands, and club as a unit along the target line away from the ball. As your hands pass your rear leg, your body starts to turn by your moving your target-side knee into your rear knee, initiating a weight shift. Your body turns, with your spine as the axis. Your head may move slightly, but with your eyes maintaining focus on the ball. Your wrists begin to cock back when the club gets about hip height; they are completely cocked by the time your hands reach a position higher than your rear shoulder. At the completion of the backswing, your trunk is completely turned, your back facing the target and your "belt buckle" facing away from the target. Your hands are higher than your rear shoulder, with the club parallel to the ground. The heel of your target-side foot is slightly off the ground.

The *forwardswing* moves the club from the top of the backswing through the ball's position. To start forwardswing, reverse the backswing's order of actions. You return your target heel to the ground first as your body begins to turn, your target knee moving laterally toward the target, beginning the weight shift back to even distribution. As the weight shift completes, your arms, hands, and club swing down as a unit. When your arms and club reach about hip height, your wrists begin to uncock (straighten out) your arms continuing to swing down. Your wrists are completely uncocked at the point of contact. Your wrists immediately begin recocking the other way, though, as your arms continue to swing through to the follow-through.

The *follow-through* is the natural completion of the forwardswing. Its point of termination is usually a momentary pause at the end of the full swing motion. The position of the follow-through is a balanced and relaxed mirror image of the "top" (farthest position) of the backswing. Your arms and hands are over your target shoulder now, with your wrist cocked. Your rear knee has moved toward your target knee, completing a weight shift toward the target. Your hips are rotated so that the "belt buckle" is facing the target, and the heel of your rear foot is slightly off the ground.

Follow all three phases of the golf swing shown in Figure 1.3. Remember that it is necessary to first learn the full swing motion without a club or ball.

Figure 1.3 Keys to Success:
Full Swing Motion
Without a Club

Preparation Phase

Setup

1. Feet shoulder width
2. Stand on imaginary line
3. Square foot alignment
4. Square hip alignment
5. Square shoulder alignment
6. Weight even on both feet
7. Bend from hips
8. Posture with flat back, eyes over hands
9. Arms hang relaxed
10. Palms of hands facing each other
11. Weight forward, midsteps to balls of feet

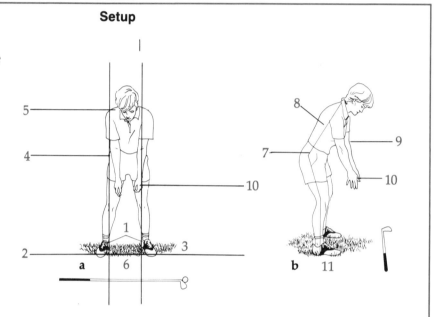

Execution Phase

Backswing

1. Arms and hands start as unit

2. Weight shifts to rear
3. Target knee touches rear knee
4. Thumbs turn away from target and up

5. Hips turn to rear
6. Back to target (belt buckle to rear)
7. Target heel rises off ground slightly
8. Hands higher than rear shoulder

Forwardswing

f   g   h   i

1. Weight shifts to target side
2. Target heel returns to ground
3. Arms and hands start down as unit
4. Hips turn back to target line
5. Thumbs return to target line (wrists uncock)

6. Arms and hands extend through bottom of swing
7. Wrists recocked at hip level (thumbs point up)
8. Weight shifts toward target
9. Rear knee moves to target knee
10. Hips turn toward target

Follow-Through Phase

j

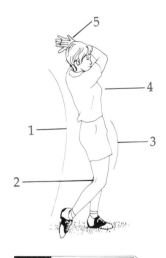

1. Weight on target side
2. Rear knee touches target knee
3. Hips face target (belt buckle toward target)
4. Chest toward target
5. Arms and hands higher than target shoulder
6. Balanced ending

Detecting Errors in
the Swing Motion Without a Club

The desired posture and swing motion is easier to recognize when compared to undesired techniques. The most common errors are presented below, along with suggestions on how to correct them.

ERROR

CORRECTION

1. You sit too far back on heels (can tap toes without losing balance).

1. Bend forward from top of thighs (see Figure 1.3b). Center weight over midsteps to balls of feet (tap heels, not toes).

2. On backswing, weight stays on target side, does not shift to rear side.

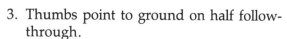

2. Shift weight to rear side by moving target knee into rear knee (see Figure 1.3c).

3. Thumbs point to ground on half follow-through.

3. Turn arms and hands as they swing downward through ball; thumbs should point to sky at follow-through (see Figure 1.3f and i).

Full Swing Motion Drills Without a Club

1. Posture Drill

Practice taking the desired posture by holding a club vertically along your spine and below your waist, then slowly bending forward from the top of your thighs. When the club comes off your back, you have bent forward too far.

Correct   Incorrect

Success Goal = 10 repetitions with club down back and correct posture

Your Score = (#) _____ repetitions

2. Body Rotation Drill

To feel your body rotate and your weight shift, take your setup position. With both hands, hold a club behind your neck and across your shoulders, the club shaft pointing toward an imaginary target. Practice the torso and leg movement of the full swing motion so that on the backswing, one club end points forward; then, at the end of the forwardswing, the opposite end points forward over the position of the ball.

Success Goal = 15 total body rotations

   5 rotations, eyes open

   5 rotations, eyes closed

   5 rotations, eyes open again

Your Score =

   (#) _____ rotations, eyes open

   (#) _____ rotations, eyes closed

   (#) _____ rotations, eyes open

3. Elephant Trunk Swing Drill or Pendulum Swing

Take your setup posture and let your arms hang forward, palms facing each other. Practice a full body turn, including the leg actions of moving your target side knee into your rear knee on the backswing, and your rear knee into your forward knee on the forwardswing (see Figure 1.3).

Success Goal = 10 full body turns with correct form

Your Score = (#) _____ turns

4. Arm Swing and Turn Drill

Find a partner to cooperate with in this drill. Lightly hold your partner's head with your hand from in front. As your partner executes a full swing, feel the motion around your partner's fixed center. Trade places.

Success Goal = 10 repetitions feeling partner's turning around fixed center

Your Score = (#) _____ repetitions

5. Wheel Image Drill

To help conceptualize the swing turn, visualize your head as the hub of a wheel and your arms as spokes. Also visualize your body swinging around an imaginary, fixed rod runing down your back.
   Close your eyes as you practice your full swing motion and visualize your body as described.

Success Goal = 10 swings with visualizations and correct form

Your Score = (#) _____ swings

Full Swing Motion Without a Club
Keys to Success Checklist

You have been testing yourself by attaining each of this first step's Success Goals. Next ask your teacher, your coach, or another trained observer to qualitatively (subjectively) evaluate your technique according to the checklist below. Ask this person to check off each item seen in your swing.

Preparation Phase

Setup

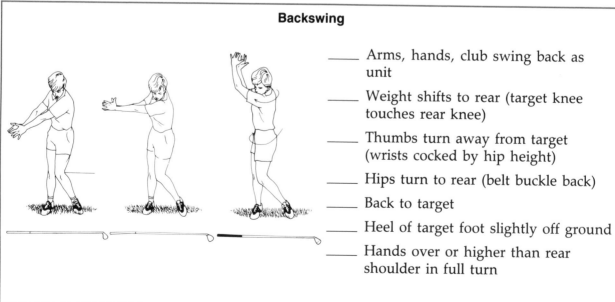

_____ Arms extended, palms together

_____ Feet shoulder width apart

_____ Weight evenly distributed

_____ Foot alignment square to target line (toes on imaginary line parallel to target line)

_____ Hips square to target line

_____ Shoulders square to target line

_____ Bends forward from hips

_____ Posture with flat back and eyes over hands

_____ Arms hang relaxed

_____ Weight forward, midstep to balls of feet

Execution Phase

Backswing

_____ Arms, hands, club swing back as unit

_____ Weight shifts to rear (target knee touches rear knee)

_____ Thumbs turn away from target (wrists cocked by hip height)

_____ Hips turn to rear (belt buckle back)

_____ Back to target

_____ Heel of target foot slightly off ground

_____ Hands over or higher than rear shoulder in full turn

Forwardswing

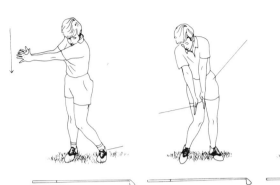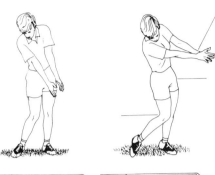

_____ Weight shifts to target side

_____ Target heel down

_____ Hips return to square

_____ Arms, hands swing down

_____ Wrists uncocked at hip level (thumbs return to point at target line)

_____ Arms, hands extended at contact with ball

_____ Hands recock at target-side hip level

_____ Weight shifts toward target

_____ Rear knee turns, touches target knee

_____ Hips turn to target (belt buckle turns toward target)

Follow-Through Phase

_____ Swing continues smoothly

_____ Arms, hands continue until hands higher than target shoulder

_____ Hips face target

_____ Chest to target

_____ Holds position at end to check for balance

_____ Weight on target side

_____ Rear knee to target knee

Step 2 Setup

The second basic golf skill to learn is the setup position for the full swing using a club and a ball. This is the ready position for every swing. As you learn the different golf shots in later steps, there will be only slight modifications of the full swing setup.

WHY IS THE
SETUP POSITION IMPORTANT?

The setup position is the foundation upon which your golf swing is built. Proper posture and relationship to the club and the ball must be consistently attained. The swing depends upon these starting points. The setup is a fundamental skill and should be practiced just like any other skill.

Consistency in your setup position helps you develop a more repeatable swing. Frequent practice will program you to take the correct setup position and grip on whatever club you select. When variations in the setup occur, the resulting swing motion is not as effective in producing the desired shot distance and direction.

HOW TO EXECUTE
THE SETUP POSITION

The setup position has seven components: (a) stance, (b) posture, (c) weight distribution, (d) body alignment, (e) grip, (f) ball position, and (g) clubface alignment. In Step 1 you practiced the first four components (a through d) as you went through the full swing motion. Now let's add the club and ball to practice the ball positioning, the grip, and clubface align-

ment. Be sure to review the Keys to Success in Step 1 (see Figure 1.3).

For the full swing using an iron, position the ball in the center relative to your stance. For a wood, place the ball about 3 inches to the target side of center. This difference is due to the lengths of the clubs and the intended angle of contacting the ball. The wood is designed to sweep the ground or contact the ball with a shallow angle, whereas the irons contact the ball with a more downward angle of the club.

The grip position now presented is called the *overlapping neutral grip* (see Figure 2.1). To grip the club, place one hand on the club at a time, beginning with your target hand. The clubface should be facing the target. Place your target hand on the club, the back of your hand facing the target. Position the club grip diagonally across your palm and fingers (see Figure 2.1b), then close your hand. Your thumb should rest just to the rear side of the club. Looking down at your grip, you should see two knuckles. There should be a V formed by your index finger and thumb, pointing to the rear side of your chin.

To position your rear hand on the club, grip the club in your target hand and hold the club in front of you (Figure 2.1d). Place your rear hand on the club with the palm of your rear hand facing the target. Hold the club in the fingers of your rear hand, the little finger of your rear hand resting on the index finger of your target hand. Your thumb should rest just to the target side of the club with one knuckle visible. There should be a V formed by your index finger and thumb, pointing just to the rear side of your chin, which all matches the V of your target hand.

Figure 2.1 Keys to Success:
   Grip

**Target
Hand**

a

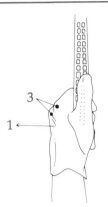

1. Back of hand to target

b

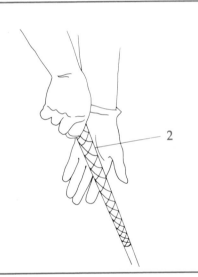

2. Club diagonally across
   palm and fingers

c

3. Two knuckles visible
4. V to rear side of chin

**Rear
Hand**

d

1. Palm of hand to target
2. Club in fingers
3. Little finger rests on target hand index finger

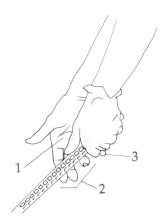

e

4. One knuckle visible
5. V to rear side of chin

The club should be aligned behind the ball in a position square to the target. To take the setup position with either a wood or an iron, grip the club in both hands. Stand erect with your feet together. Extend your arms, allowing them to rest lightly on your chest. Keeping your back straight, bend from the top of your thighs to a point where the club touches the ground behind the ball.

For an iron, move your target foot toward the target about 8 inches and your rear foot away from the target about 8 inches. This produces a ball position in the center of your stance for the iron (see Figure 2.2a).

For a wood, move your target foot about 2 inches toward the target and your rear foot about 14 inches away from the target. This produces a stance that is shoulder width (approximately 16 inches). The ball position is shifted toward the target relative to your body,

the center of your body behind the ball (see Figure 2.2b).

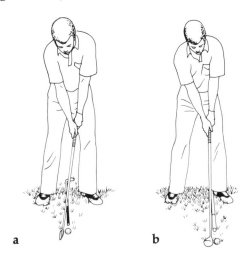

Figure 2.2 (a) Ball position is center of stance for irons; (b) ball position is 3 inches to target side of stance center for woods.

The position of the clubface when it is resting behind the ball is referred to as the *clubface alignment*. For almost all shots in golf, the clubface should be perpendicular to the target line, the desired line of flight of the ball. As you become more advanced, you may wish to vary this position. For now, though, be sure that your clubface is square to the target. It is also important that the club is resting flat on the ground. Every club has a relatively flat bottom surface (the sole), designed to rest on the ground. Be sure your clubface is both square to the target and that the club's sole is resting flat on the ground (see Figure 2.3).

Figure 2.3 Keys to Success: Setup

Preparation Phase

Setup

1. Neutral grip
2. Feet shoulder width apart
3. Square foot alignment
4. Square hip alignment
5. Square shoulder alignment
6. Weight even over both feet
7. Posture over ball
8. Weight forward, mid-step to balls of feet
9. Ball position with iron: center of stance; wood: 3 inches to target side of center
10. Blade square (perpendicular to target line)

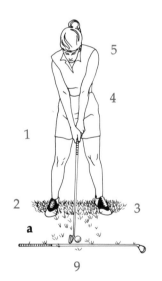
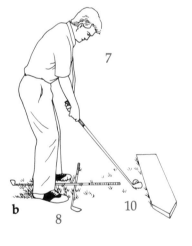

Detecting Setup Errors

Constantly checking your setup position helps you develop consistency in your swing. The most common errors that are found in the setup are described below, along with suggestions for their correction.

ERROR

CORRECTION

1. Your grip is turned, with Vs formed by index fingers and thumbs pointing toward rear shoulder.

1. Move hands more toward target side so Vs are pointing just to rear side of chin at first (see Figure 2.1c).

2. In setup position, arms stretch out too far, so that a plumb line from eyes would fall onto forearms.

2. Move arms closer to body to position where plumb line would fall on hands.

ERROR   **CORRECTION**

3. You position ball too far forward, off your target heel with an iron.

3. Practice setting up with an iron by placing a club on ground in middle of stance.

4. You sit back in stance as if you were sitting on stool or tilting backward; you can tap your toes easily.

4. Move shoulders forward so body weight is over the midstep to balls of feet; thus, you can tap heels, not toes.

Setup Drills

1. Grip Drill

Practice taking your grip with your eyes closed. Hold your arms straight out in front of your chest, the club up in the air. Then open your eyes. Are your palms facing each other, with a palm-and-finger grip in your target hand and the fingers of your rear hand covering the target hand thumb?

Success Goal = 10 practice grips with all checkpoints correct

Your Score = (#) _____ grips

2. Weight Distribution Drill

First take your proper stance. Now feel an undesired setup position by leaning back as if you were sitting on a stool. Do your arms feel as relaxed as in the desired position? Next tip too far forward so your weight is on the balls and toes of your feet. Tap your heels on the ground. Now find the middle position. Repeat these three positions—back, forward, and balanced.

Success Goal = 3 cycles taking proper stance, then shifting weight backward, too far forward, and back to ideal stance

　3 setup positions forward

　3 setup positions back

　3 setup positions balanced

Your Score =

　(#) _____ setups forward

　(#) _____ setups back

　(#) _____ setups balanced

3. Walk Away Alignment Drill

Practice your setup position by starting from well behind the ball. Pick an imaginary target, then walk up and take your setup over the ball. Now lay your club on the ground, touching the tips of your toes. Walk back behind ball and look at club to determine whether your toes were parallel to the target line. Pick different targets and repeat.

Success Goal = 10 consecutive correct parallel alignments, each attempt directed at a different target

Your Score = (#) _____ parallel alignments

4. Arm Hang Drill

After taking your setup, release your grip on the club and let it fall away. Let your arms relax; note whether they remain hanging straight down or swing in toward or away from your body. If your arms swing out, you are too close to the ball. If they fall in toward your body, you are too far away from the ball.

Success Goal = 10 arm hangs demonstrating correct relationship to ball

Your Score = (#) _____ arm hangs

5. Setup Sequence Drill

Sight a target from behind your ball. Select a club and take your grip while standing behind the ball and looking at the target. Walk up to the ball and set the clubface perpendicular to the target line. Set your feet and take your proper posture and alignment.

Success Goal = 10 setups in correct sequence

Your Score = (#) _____ setups

Setup
Keys to Success Checklist

In order to be sure that you are taking the proper setup position, ask your teacher, your coach, or another trained observer to evaluate your stance and grip objectively. The following checklist can assist in this process of judging your progress through Steps 1 and 2. Each item should be checked as it is observed.

Preparation Phase

Grip

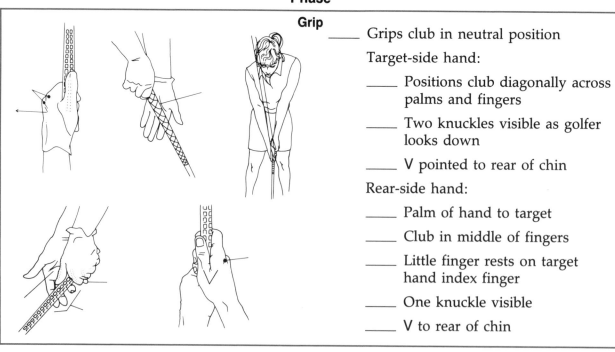

_____ Grips club in neutral position

Target-side hand:

_____ Positions club diagonally across palms and fingers

_____ Two knuckles visible as golfer looks down

_____ V pointed to rear of chin

Rear-side hand:

_____ Palm of hand to target

_____ Club in middle of fingers

_____ Little finger rests on target hand index finger

_____ One knuckle visible

_____ V to rear of chin

Stance

_____ Feet shoulder width apart

_____ Weight evenly distributed

_____ Foot alignment square to target line

_____ Hips square to target line

_____ Shoulders square to target line

_____ Posture with flat back and eyes over hands

_____ Weight forward, midstep to balls of feet

Ball position:

_____ Iron: near center of stance

_____ Wood: 3 inches to target side of center

_____ Blade of club square to target line

Step 3 Applying the Full Swing With Irons and Woods

The full swing motion and the setup position you have been practicing are the foundation for your golf swing. In this step, you apply the setup and swing motion to actually hit golf balls with irons and woods. In the steps that follow (Steps 4 through 9), you will learn to apply the setup and the full swing motion to execute a variety of shots needed to play golf.

WHY IS THE FULL SWING MOTION WITH IRONS AND WOODS IMPORTANT?

On the golf course, the full swing motion is used for about 50% of the shots. Therefore, if you can master this one motion, you will be halfway to being a good golfer!

The game of golf lets you use a single, consistent swinging motion for most types of shots. Because the design of the golf club largely determines the trajectory and distance of the shot, the golfer carries a set of 14 clubs that vary in shape and length. There are many different clubs to be used on any one hole, depending on how far you must hit the ball, the trajectory needed, and the situation from which the shot starts (e.g., tall grass or sand). Yet, the basic full swing remains the same for every shot. In contrast, the pace of racket sports such as tennis requires that you play all the shots in a point with a single racket. As a result, for different types of shots, the racket stroke varies considerably. Since the golfer can switch to the ideal club for the shot, there is no need to vary the stroke. Having such a wide selection of clubs allows the golfer to rely and concentrate on a single, consistent swinging motion for most types of shots.

As discussed in more detail in the equipment section, each club is designed to hit the ball in a way that makes it fly higher or lower and cover shorter or longer distances. In general, the higher the number of a club, the higher the ball's trajectory and the shorter the

overall distance. The trajectories depicted in Figure 3.1 illustrate how the various clubs produce different flight distances and trajectories even though you hit every shot with the same full swing. Compare the distances and trajectories of the 3-wood (sometimes used in place of a driver) and the 9-iron (a short iron). The 3-wood hits the ball farther over a lower trajectory; in contrast, the 9-iron makes the ball fly higher for a shorter distance.

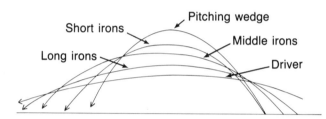

Figure 3.1 Ball flight trajectories produced with a full swing, depending on the club.

No two golfers using a given club hit the ball the same distance, because each person does not have the same skill or strength in accelerating the club through the swing (as will be discussed in Step 4). For example, in a group of four beginning golfers, if all four were the same distance from the pin, each player might hit a different club. Some might hit woods and others irons, depending on their individual swing characteristics (i.e., how fast and straight they swing the club) and their preferences for using one club over another. In each case, though, a full swing motion would be applied.

HOW TO EXECUTE THE FULL SWING MOTION WITH IRONS AND WOODS

The same full swing motion and basic setup position are used for both irons and woods. The only difference between hitting irons and woods is the ball placement. For irons the ball is positioned within 1 or 2 inches of the center of your stance. For woods the ball is about 3 or 4 inches from the center, toward the target side. Your ideal ball position can be found by taking your setup position with the club touching the ground in the center of your stance for an iron, and just to the target side of center for the longer woods. Then take one or two practice swings without a ball. Watch where the club consistently contacts the ground with each swing. This is the bottom of your swing arc, where the club will contact the bottom of the ball. This is your ball position.

As you are learning the full swing motion, your ball contact and ball flight direction may be inconsistent. Do not worry about that for now. Concentrate on feeling the arm swing motion. Allow your body to respond to the swing. The motion of your arms and hands swinging the club is rhythmic and free, with your body rotation and weight shift responding to the arm swing. The sequence of movements presented in Step 1 and the Keys to Success in Figure 3.2 should flow smoothly and uninterrupted by any sudden surge of power or forced effort.

Imagine a child swinging in the park. The chains of the swing represent your arms; the child and seat, your hands and club. The upward motion is smooth but gradually slows down. There is an almost imperceptible pause at the height of the upward motion. As the swing starts back on the forward motion, there is a gradual acceleration that continues *through* the lowest part of the swing's arc as the swing comes close to the ground and then begins to swing upward. There the swing begins a natural, gradual deceleration. Imagine that your swing feels like the rhythmic swing in the park.

Figure 3.2 Keys to Success: The Full Swing With Clubs

Preparation Phase

1. Neutral grip
2. Feet shoulder width
3. Square foot alignment
4. Square hip alignment
5. Square shoulder alignment
6. Weight even over both feet
7. Posture over ball, and flat back
8. Weight forward, mid-step to balls of feet
9. Ball position with irons: center of stance; woods: target side of center
10. Blade square (perpendicular to target line)

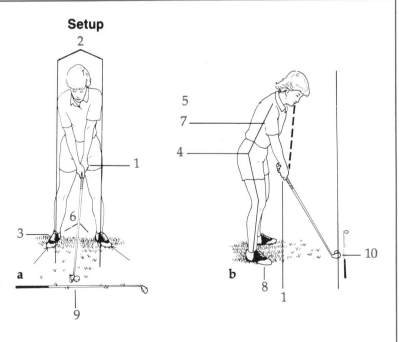

**Execution
Phase**

Backswing

c

d

e

1. Arms, hands, club start as unit

2. Weight shifts to rear (target knee touches rear knee)
3. Wrists cock at hip level

4. Hips turn to rear
5. Back to target
6. Club parallel to ground
7. Hands over rear shoulder

Forwardswing

f

g

h

1. Weight shifts to target side
2. Arms, hands, club start down as unit

3. Wrists uncock at hip level
4. Hips return to square
5. Target heel down

6. Arms, hands, club extended at contact
7. Target knee toward target
8. Rear knee toward target knee

**Follow-Through
Phase**

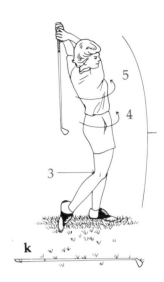

1. Wrists recock at target hip level
2. Hips turned to target

3. Weight on target side (rear knee touches target knee)

4. Hips face target
5. Chest to target
6. Balanced ending

Detecting Full Swing Errors With Irons and Woods

The most common problems in developing your full swing are made obvious by improper contact with the ball. These errors are listed below, along with suggestions on how to correct them.

ERROR

CORRECTION

1. Club hits ground behind ball.

1a. Keep arms swinging through ball as your weight shifts.

b. Maintain posture through impact.

c. Review arm swing drills in Step 1.

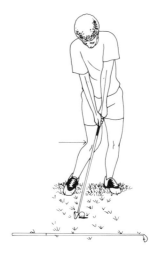

2. Club hits top of ball.

2a. Keep arms extended toward ground on forwardswing.

b. Check arm extension as wrists uncock toward ball.

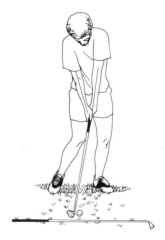

ERROR

CORRECTION

3. You hit ball off toe of club.

3. Maintain posture over ball: Avoid "standing up" or shifting weight back onto heels during forward-swing.

4. You *shank* ball, hitting it off heel of club.

4. Check setup position for relaxed arms, rather than incorrectly having arms stretched too far away from body or leaning forward beyond ball (see correction 3).

ERROR **CORRECTION**

5. Lack of shot distance comes with full swings due to not turning hips.

5. Take practice swings to feel full body turn and arm swing during both backswing and follow-through. Think "belt buckle back and belt buckle through."

6. Ball travels straight but ends up off-target.

6. Check your alignment using Walk Away Alignment Drill in Step 2 to check for square alignment; perform Pendulum Drill in Step 1 to check on arm swing.

7. You swing and miss ball (called a *whiff*).

7a. Check that posture remains same throughout swing.

b. Maintain arm extension through forwardswing.

Full Swing Drills

1. Wide Whoosher Drill

To feel the freedom of the arm swing, hold a club upside down in your target hand just above the *hosel* (the socket in the clubhead for the shaft). Turn the club parallel to the ground, the grip pointing away from an imaginary target. Grip the club shaft with the fingers of your rear hand, palm up, about 1 foot from your target hand.

Take setup position with club parallel to ground. Make your full swing motion to the top of the backswing. Let go with your rear hand and pull down and through with your target-side arm and hand. The club should make a swishing or whooshing sound. (If not, you are not accelerating the swing of the club fast enough through the ball.)

Success Goal = 10 swings with a loud whooshing sound

Your Score = (#) _____ swings

2. Wheel Drill Without a Ball

To get a feel for the pendulum motion of the full arm swing, imagine that your arms and hands together gripping a club are the spoke of a wheel. The length of your backswing and forwardswing are represented on each side of the wheel with the numbers 1–5. Zero is the ball and the setup position of the clubhead.

Practice swinging a 5- or 7-iron in a very short arc, from backswing position 1 to forwardswing position 1. Allow the club to brush the ground on each forwardswing. Now swing it 2-to-2, 3-to-3, 4-to-4, and 5-to-5. Be sure your swing is the same length on the backswing as on the forwardswing. Sense how the feel of the swing matches how long it is. With your eyes closed, establish this same feel.

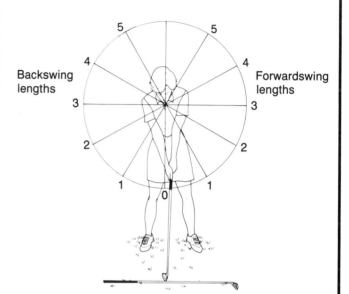

Backswing lengths

Forwardswing lengths

Success Goal =

   a. 10 total swings with a 5- or 7-iron

       2 swings, 1-to-1 swing length (no wrist cock)

       2 swings, 2-to-2 swing length (no wrist cock)

       2 swings, 3-to-3 swing length (wrists cock)

       2 swings, 4-to-4 swing length (wrists cock)

       2 swings, 5-to-5 swing length (wrists cock)

   b. 10 total swings repeating (a), with *eyes closed*

Your Score =

   a. (#) _____ total swings with eyes open

   b. (#) _____ total swings with eyes closed

3. Wheel Drill With a Ball

a. Visualize the wheel practiced with the previous drill. Using a 5- or 7-iron and a ball placed on a tee (about one finger's width high), hit balls with each of the swing lengths. Match the feel of the swing with the resultant distance that the ball travels.

b. With a ball not teed, repeat (a). Be sure the ball is sitting on top of the ground or on grass—not in a divot hole.

Success Goal =

a. 25 total swings, ball elevated on a tee

　　5 swings, 1-to-1 swing length

　　5 swings, 2-to-2 swing length

　　5 swings, 3-to-3 swing length

　　5 swings, 4-to-4 swing length

　　5 swings, 5-to-5 swing length

b. 25 total swings, ball resting on ground (no tee)

　　5 swings, 1-to-1 swing length

　　5 swings, 2-to-2 swing length

　　5 swings, 3-to-3 swing length

　　5 swings, 4-to-4 swing length

　　5 swings, 5-to-5 swing length

Your Score =

Swing length	Swing (goal N = 5 each)
a. Ball on tee	
1-to-1	(#) _____ swings
2-to-2	(#) _____ swings
3-to-3	(#) _____ swings
4-to-4	(#) _____ swings
5-to-5	(#) _____ swings
b. Ball on ground	
1-to-1	(#) _____ swings
2-to-2	(#) _____ swings
3-to-3	(#) _____ swings
4-to-4	(#) _____ swings
5-to-5	(#) _____ swings

4. Cocking Drill Without a Ball

This drill helps you feel the maximum wrist cock, uncock, and recock you would ever desire on the backswing or forwardswing. Take your setup position. Without swinging your arms, cock your wrists back so they point to the sky. This is the maximum wrist cock.

a. With a 7-iron, take your stance with your feet close together. Without swinging your arms, turn your thumbs away from the target, back to the ball, and then toward the target. The forearms turn as the thumbs turn.

b. Add a 3-to-3 arm swing arc, the hand action created by the cocking and uncocking of the wrists. Note the swinging sensations in your arms and hands.

c. Take your normal stance and setup with your feet shoulder width apart. Add the lower-body motion, feeling your weight shift as a response to your arm swing.

Success Goal = 30 total swings using swing cue word (as in Whooshing Drill) each time

    a. 10 swings of cocking, uncocking, and recocking wrists without swinging arms

    b. 10 swings of cocking, uncocking, and recocking wrists, with arms moving 3-to-3 swing length

    c. 10 swings of cocking, uncocking, and recocking wrists, and using arms and lower body motion

Your Score =

    a. (#) _____ swings, wrists only

    b. (#) _____ swings, wrists and arms only

    c. (#) _____ swings, entire body

5. Cocking Drill With a Ball

Repeat the cocking drill described in the previous drill, only now hitting a golf ball on a tee. Practice your swing motion with the cocking, uncocking, and recocking of your wrists. Think of the ball as merely "getting in the way" of your swing. Use a cue word such as "release" or "swish" each time you do the cocking drill. Note the differences in feel and distance the ball travels when you hit with no arm swing, with arms only, and with arms with body action.

Success Goal = 30 total swings using a cue word and a teed ball

   a. 10 swings of cocking, uncocking, and recocking wrists without swinging arms

   b. 10 swings of cocking, uncocking, and recocking wrists, with arms moving 3-to-3 swing length

   c. 10 swings of cocking, uncocking, and recocking wrists, using arms and lower body motion

Your Score =

   a. (#) _____ swings, wrists only

   b. (#) _____ swings, wrists and arms only

   c. (#) _____ swings, entire body

6. Distance Drill

It is important for you to be able to match how a swing feels with how far the golf ball travels. Ideally, you want to hit the ball as far as you can with consistent control. You can change either the speed of your swing or the club you select to achieve a specific, desired distance less than your maximum. As you are developing your swing, distance control may be inconsistent. However, using this drill provides you with a system for measuring your progress as well as a distance assessment for each club.

Place 7 targets in a field at 10-yard intervals beginning at 90 yards away from the ball and ending at 160 yards. Using a 5-iron, practice hitting balls toward the targets. Use an alignment club to assure direction; carefully take your setup position with each swing. Determine the average distance you hit your 5-iron; most of your shots should cluster near the average. Continue this process with each club (woods and irons). You may need to adjust your yardage markers longer or shorter to fit your distance needs. This drill is best used with irons and woods on separate days.

Success Goal = consistent distance 50% or more of the time (this percentage will increase with practice)

10 swings, 5-iron

10 swings, 7-iron

10 swings, 9-iron

10 swings, 3-iron

10 swings, 7-wood

10 swings, 5-wood

10 swings, 3-wood

Your Score = distance hit (hit in club order on chart)

Shot	Irons				Woods		
	5	7	9	3	7	5	3
1	___	___	___	___	___	___	___
2	___	___	___	___	___	___	___
3	___	___	___	___	___	___	___
4	___	___	___	___	___	___	___
5	___	___	___	___	___	___	___
6	___	___	___	___	___	___	___
7	___	___	___	___	___	___	___
8	___	___	___	___	___	___	___
9	___	___	___	___	___	___	___
10	___	___	___	___	___	___	___
Total	___	___	___	___	___	___	___
Average	___	___	___	___	___	___	___

7. One-Leg Toe Drill

It is important to maintain your balance through your golf swing. Select any iron and take your regular full swing setup. Maintaining proper posture, place your rear foot directly behind your target-side foot. Place *only* the toe of your rear-side foot on the ground. Practice making swings using the 3-to-3 swing length from this position. Be sure to let your wrists cock, uncock, and recock. Notice how your body and hands feel. Be sure not to fall out of balance.

Success Goal = 30 total swings while staying in balance

10 swings, without ball

10 swings, ball on tee

10 swings, ball on ground

Your Score =

(#) _____ swings, without ball

(#) _____ swings, ball on tee

(#) _____ swings, ball on ground

Full Swing With Irons and Woods
Keys to Success Checklist

You have been quantitatively testing yourself by attaining each of the Step 3 Success Goals. Now ask your teacher, coach, or another trained observer to qualitatively evaluate your technique according to the checklist below. Each item should be checked as it is observed. Be sure to note the ball position differences with irons as opposed to woods.

**Preparation
Phase**

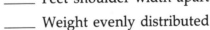

Setup

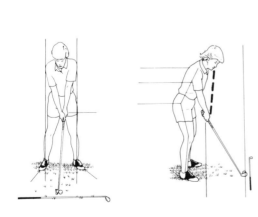

_____ Grips club in neutral position (Vs in grip pointing to rear of chin)

_____ Feet shoulder width apart

_____ Weight evenly distributed

_____ Foot alignment square to target line

_____ Hips square to target line

_____ Shoulders square to target line

_____ Posture with flat back and eyes over hands

_____ Weight forward, midstep to balls of feet

_____ Ball position with irons: near center of stance; with woods: target side of center

_____ Blade of club square to target

Execution
Phase

Backswing

_____ Arms, hands, and club swing back as unit

_____ Weight shifts to rear (target knee touches rear knee)

_____ Wrists cocked at hip level

_____ Hips turn to rear (belt buckle back)

_____ Backswing length 5

_____ Heel of target foot off ground slightly

_____ Hands over rear shoulder in full turn

_____ Club parallel to ground

_____ Back to target

Forwardswing

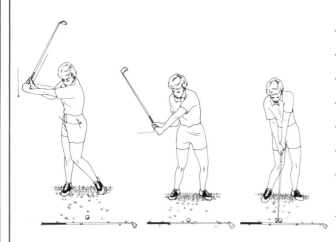

_____ Weight shifts to target side

_____ Target heel down

_____ Target knee toward target

_____ Hips return to square

_____ Arms, hands, club swing down

_____ Wrists uncocked at hip level

_____ Arms, club, hands extended at contact with ball

_____ Rear knee turns towards target knee

Follow-Through
Phase

_____ Swing continues smoothly; wrists recock at hip level

_____ Arms, hands, club continue until hands are higher than target shoulder

_____ Hips face target

_____ Forwardswing length 5

_____ Chest to target

_____ Holds position at end to check for balance

_____ Weight on target side (rear knee touches target knee)

Step 4 Learning From the Flight of Your Golf Ball

All sport skills have inherent feedback mechanisms for telling the performer what is happening with the skill. In basketball, the ball either goes through the hoop or is shot with too much or too little force or is off-target to the side. Similarly, in golf the flight of the ball gives you information about your swing. The direction the ball travels through the air is important, not simply its distance. For example, your golf ball could go 200 yards; the shot's distance is good, yet overall it would be a bad shot if the ball landed 20 yards to the right of the target due either to an error in the path of the ball or to the way it spins and curves through space.

WHY IS IT IMPORTANT TO LEARN FROM THE FLIGHT OF YOUR BALL?

The flight of your golf ball is your "teacher" when you practice and play. Most of the fundamental swing errors that golfers of all ability levels experience can be identified through understanding which errors cause particular ball flight patterns. Learning to observe and interpret your ball flight is your key to becoming a more successful golfer. Your practice sessions and course play will be more effective and efficient because you can self-correct, improving your swing fundamentals.

The best way to understand fundamental errors is to watch the ball flight after you have hit a shot. If your golf ball goes in a straight line with only a slight curve to the right or left, you have a good start. If your ball lands too short or past the target, you probably are not swinging the club at the appropriate speed or have selected the wrong club. If your ball flies in a straight line but goes to the left or right of the target, you have made what is called a *path error*. On the other hand, if your ball curves excessively while in the air, your shot is referred to as either a *hook* or a *slice*, depend-

ing on the direction of the curve. These curving flight paths are the results of errors in the way the face of the club strikes the ball. These errors are clues to identifying certain problems with your swing. The possible combinations of ball flight paths and curvatures are illustrated in Figure 4.1.

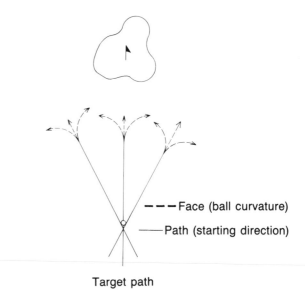

- - - Face (ball curvature)

—— Path (starting direction)

Target path

Figure 4.1 Nine possible ball flight patterns.

When learning to play golf, it is important to train yourself to see the ball flight and remember what causes the characteristics you observe. It is also important to remember that you should focus on a good swing first, striving for smoothness and speed. You can then learn to control the direction and angle of approach of the club to the ball. The faster the club is traveling when it squarely contacts the ball, the farther the ball goes. In fact, research has shown that a well-controlled speed of about 65% of the maximum swing speed optimizes both speed and accuracy. So, don't try to "kill" the ball, but swing at a relatively fast rate—about 65% of your fastest swing.

HOW TO LEARN FROM THE FLIGHT OF YOUR BALL

In order to learn from the flight of your ball, you must remember to do two important things: Always aim at a specific target and be sure to use a consistent setup position so that you know that you are aligned with the target.

When you observe your ball flight, determine whether it starts out traveling in a straight line or curves in the air from the very beginning. If you are a right-handed golfer and your shot curves dramatically to the right, it is a *slice*; to the left, it is a *hook*. If you are left-handed, your slice goes to the left, your hook to the right. Hooks or slices result from the clubhead being at an angle to a side when it meets the ball, thereby imparting spin to the ball. A slice is the result of an open clubface, and a hook is the result of a closed clubface.

Sometimes a golf ball travels in a straight line but still lands off to the right or left of the target. If you were lined up straight at the target when you hit the ball but it landed off-target, it is probably because the club traveled in a path that pointed in that direction. This is quite similar to a right-handed baseball batter who hits the ball over first base or pulls it over third base, even though the batter is lined up aiming over the pitcher toward second base. When a right-handed golfer *pushes* the ball, it lands to the right of the target because the clubhead has been pushed in that direction during the swing. On the other hand, if a right-handed golfer *pulls* the club across the normal target line, the ball lands to the left of the target. (For a left-handed golfer, a ball traveling straight but landing to the left is a push, whereas one landing to the right is a pull.)

It is important to realize that the only thing that directly affects the flight of the ball is the way the club contacts it at impact. There are five club factors that affect the way energy is imparted from club to ball, which are discussed in this step: speed of clubhead at impact, path on which the club is swung, position of clubface at impact, squareness of contact of clubface with ball, and angle of approach of clubface. Each of these elements may be affected by your setup position in relation to the target.

The golf swing is fundamentally a very simple arc motion. If you think of your arms and the club as a pendulum, the swing is a very understandable motion. The position and speed of the club at the moment it contacts the ball determine exactly how far the ball goes. The path on which the club swings determines the starting direction, whereas the angle of the face of the club determines the spin imparted to the ball. Because the club controls the ball and you control the club, you can become your own self-corrector by understanding some simple ball flight influences that are summarized in Figure 4.2.

Figure 4.2 Keys to Success: The Flight of the Ball

Distance Influenced By

1. Squareness of contact
2. Fast club speed
3. Appropriate angle of approach
4. Squareness of clubface alignment

Direction Influenced By

Curving Balls (slice or hook)

1. Clubface not square
   a. Open tends to slice
   b. Closed tends to hook

Off-Target Balls (push or pull)

1. Alignment not square at setup (aims off-target)
2. Swing path not square at impact

Detecting Errors by Watching the Flight of the Ball

There are two primary types of errors that can be observed in the flight of the ball: directional and distance errors. These can be summarized as follows:

1. The direction is primarily affected by
   • the aiming (alignment) of your body and the clubface at setup,
   • the path upon which you swing the club,
   • the position of the clubface when it contacts the ball.

2. The distance the ball travels is primarily affected by
   • how squarely you hit the ball on the clubface,
   • how fast the club is traveling when it hits the ball,
   • the club's angle of approach when it hits the ball.

The most fundamental problem that causes errors in the landing direction of the ball is poor alignment in the setup. In addition to such a basic aiming problem, there may also be problems with the path of the club when you swing it or with the angle of the clubface when it strikes the ball.

The way in which the clubface is aligned with the path of the swing is another important factor in the resultant landing direction of the ball. The angle of the clubface when it strikes the ball determines the spin on the ball. Just like spin on a curveball in baseball, spin affects the way the golf ball travels through space. The face of the club should be square at contact. If it is open, a slice results; if closed, a hook.

In order to tell what happened when your ball lands off-target to the right or left, you may need to ask yourself these two questions:

Did the ball travel straight, but to the right or left of target?
  If so, it is likely to be a path or alignment error.

Did the ball curve excessively while in the air?
  If so, it is likely that a clubface error caused the excessive ball spin.

DIRECTION ERROR: PATH

1. Ball travels straight but lands left or right of target, a path error due to an alignment problem.
   Explanation. Directional errors are primarily caused by one of two problems:
   • Lack of square alignment
   • Club swung on a path not aligned to target

CORRECTION

1. Adjust alignment of body to square position. Stance should be parallel to target. Check
   • feet,
   • hips,
   • shoulders.

DIRECTION ERROR: PATH **CORRECTION**

2. Ball lands right or left due to path on which you swing club.
   Explanation. Direction of ball flight is primarily the same as the direction in which you swing the club.

If the ball flight tends to curve more than desired in either direction, there can be two possible sources. First, check your alignment toward the target. If you are square with the target line, it is likely that the problem is due to the angle of the clubhead at impact. This angle is most often controlled by (a) your grip on the club, (b) by the wrist action, which is called the *release*, through the contact zone, or (c) club path. (These are principles discussed in the next chapter.)

2. Swing club on path to target:
   • Check alignment,
   • Use alignment of club to visualize desired path.

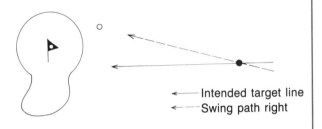

Intended target line
Swing path right

DIRECTION ERROR: CLUBFACE **CORRECTION**

3. Ball slices.
   Explanation. Angle of clubface in relation to path of swing determines sidespin imparted to ball:
   • An open clubface produces a slice.
   • A closed clubface produces a hook.
   • A square clubface produces no left or right spin.

3. Allow hands to relax and release to allow clubhead to return to square at contact.

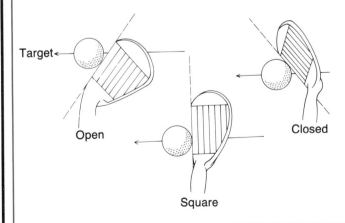

Target

Open

Square

Closed

DIRECTION ERROR: CLUBFACE   **CORRECTION**

4. Ball hooks.

   Explanation. Angle of clubface in relation to path of swing determines sidespin imparted to ball:

   • An open clubface produces a slice.
   • A closed clubface produces a hook.
   • A square clubface produces no left or right spin.

The distance that a golf ball travels is primarily dependent upon the speed of the clubhead at impact. How much force is transferred from the club to the ball at impact is affected by three things: clubhead speed, the angle of approach of the club, and the squareness of contact made by the club on the ball.

Each club is a different length and has a different clubface angle. These two factors have impact on how fast the club is moving when it contacts the ball and on the angle of the force that is imparted. In addition, it is possible to control the trajectory of the ball flight by changing the angle at which the club is swung downward at the ball and changing the

4. Arms are stopping too soon, and hands uncock early. Increase tension in hands to change timing of release; be sure hands and arms start down as a unit.

ball position. If you contact the ball above its *equator*, or centerline, it travels at a lower angle; if you contact it below its equator, the ball travels higher. This is why irons are designed to hit down on the ball and strike below its center, whereas fairway woods typically are swung in such a way as to strike the ball just after the club reaches the lowest spot in its pendular swing. Note that your setup position and the location of the ball to the target side of center for woods also facilitates this difference. In contrast, the putter is designed to hit the ball squarely in its center and is swung in an essentially straight or horizontal line.

DISTANCE ERROR   **CORRECTION**

5. Ball lands short of target, but flight looks about the right height.

   Explanation. Distance a golf ball travels depends on four things:

   • Length of swing
   • Speed of clubhead at moment of impact with ball
   • Squareness of contact made by club on ball
   • Angle of approach of club to ball

5. Increase length of swing or swing speed.

Descending (irons)

Level to slightly
ascending (fairway woods)

Level (putter)

Ascending (tee shots)

DISTANCE ERROR 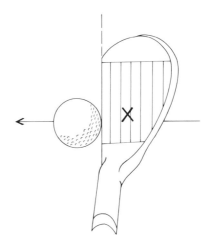 **CORRECTION**

6. Ball travels too high with an iron and lands short of target.

6. Angle of approach is too steep. Adjust angle of approach to be shallower or less steep by extending swing (making it wider on backswing and forward-swing; see explanation 5).

7. Ball seems to pop up in the air on the tee shot due to an angle of approach that is too steep.

7. Check the height of the tee to be sure it's not more than 2 inches high. Adjust angle of approach of club by extending swing (making it wider on backswing and forwardswing; see explanation 5).

8. Ball lands short of target, but swing seems about the right speed and length. **Explanation.** Each club has a *sweet spot*, also called a *centroid*, which is its center of mass extended to the club-face surface. This is the clubface point that can impart the most force to the ball, which can then travel its maximum distance. The farther away from the sweet spot the ball is hit, the more its distance and direction varies.

8. Check for square contact of clubface on ball.
   • Club selection may have to be changed.

9. Ball shoots off sharply in front of golfer due to being hit in the hosel—a "shank." Upper body falls back on forward-swing.

9. Contact ball with centroid of club by keeping proper posture over ball on forwardswing.

Ball Flight Drills

1. Long-Short Drill

To feel how much effect the speed of the swing has on the distance a ball travels, experiment with slow and fast swing speeds. Using a good setup and 5, 7, and 9 irons, hit 3 consecutive balls with the same club. Use fast swing speed so the first shot goes long, slow swing speed to make the second short, and normal swing speed to make the third land in the middle. Practice changing the speed of your swing in order to adjust the distance.

Success Goal = hitting 9 balls, varying the speeds of the swings to make the balls travel long, short, then medium distance

   a. 9-iron

   b. 5- or 7-iron

   c. Wood or long iron

Your Score = Check the distance you hit the balls when using each club

   a. 9-iron: long _____ , short _____ , medium _____

   b. 5- or 7-iron: long _____ , short _____ , medium _____

   c. Wood or long iron: long _____ , short _____ , medium _____

2. Pop-Up Drill

The trajectory of a golf ball is affected by the angle of approach of the clubhead at contact. Using one club (a 5- or 7-iron), make your shots travel higher or lower by adjusting the angle of approach of your swing or by shifting the position of the ball in the center of your stance.

Success Goal = hitting 12 total balls, making them travel at different heights by adjusting the angle of approach

  a. 3 balls hit at steep angle

  b. 3 balls hit at shallow angle

  c. 3 balls hit at normal angle

  d. 1 ball hit at steep angle

  e. 1 ball hit at shallow angle

  f. 1 ball hit at normal angle

Your Score =

  a. (#) _____ hit at steep angle

  b. (#) _____ hit at shallow angle

  c. (#) _____ hit at normal angle

  d. (#) _____ hit at steep angle

  e. (#) _____ hit at shallow angle

  f. (#) _____ hit at normal angle

3. Slice and Hook Drill

By adjusting the angle the clubface contacts the ball, make the ball either hook or slice. For a hook, use a light grip pressure to cause the clubhead to be closed at contact. For a slice, increase tension in your hands and wrists, preventing the clubhead from returning to square. This lack of wrist action causes the clubhead to remain open at contact.

Be careful not to confuse the directional errors of a push or a pull with the desired slices or hooks.

Success Goal = hitting 28 total slices and hooks by adjusting angle clubface contacts ball

a. Hit 5 slices

b. Hit 5 hooks

c. Hit 5 balls straight

d. Hit 3 slices

e. Hit 3 hooks

f. Hit 3 straight

g. Hit 1 slice

h. Hit 1 straight

i. Hit 1 hook

j. Hit 1 straight

Your Score =

a. (#) _____ slices (5)

b. (#) _____ hooks (5)

c. (#) _____ balls straight (5)

d. (#) _____ slices (3)

e. (#) _____ hooks (3)

f. (#) _____ straight (3)

g. (#) _____ slice (1)

h. (#) _____ straight (1)

i. (#) _____ hook (1)

j. (#) _____ straight (1)

4. Two-by-Four Drill

In order to check the swing path of your club, place a two-by-four piece of wood parallel to the target line. Place your ball about 2 inches in from the board and hit it. (*Note*: For safety reasons, be sure the board extends about 2 feet to the nontarget side of the ball, or substitute your golf bag for the board.)

Success Goal = hitting 15 total shots in a row (3 with each club) without touching the board during the swing

   3 shots, 5-iron

   3 shots, 7-iron

   3 shots, 9-iron

   3 shots, 3-iron

   3 shots, wood

Your Score =

   (#) _____ shots, 5-iron

   (#) _____ shots, 7-iron

   (#) _____ shots, 9-iron

   (#) _____ shots, 3-iron

   (#) _____ shots, wood

5. Bogey Challenge

With a partner, take turns playing follow-the-leader. If your partner calls for, say, a slice and then hits one, you must also hit a slice. If you fail, you receive the next letter in the word *bogey* (or another golf-related word of your choosing), as in the basketball game of Horse. Each time you miss a called shot, you receive another letter in the word. The loser is the first person to have the entire word (to have missed 5 called shots).

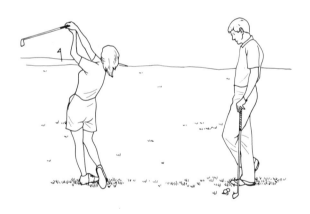

Success Goal = to avoid acquiring all letters in the word *bogey* by successfully hitting all shots your partner expects you to execute; and to attempt to call and hit shots that your partner cannot execute, therefore causing penalty letters to be picked up by partner

Your Score = penalty letters (spell) _____

Ball Flight
Keys to Success Checklist

In order to check your understanding of the errors that affect ball flight, attempt to execute each of the following successfully at least 3 out of 5 times, using a 5-iron. Place a check in the blank for each successful attempt. Once you can execute these types of shots when you want to, you can avoid them when they appear as errors. This form of variable practice has been shown to be very effective in learning to focus on your body movement. Asterisks denote errors.

____ ____ ____ ____ ____ Slice

____ ____ ____ ____ ____ Hook

____ ____ ____ ____ ____ Push

____ ____ ____ ____ ____ Pull

____ ____ ____ ____ ____ Top the ball

____ ____ ____ ____ ____ Hit ball at very bottom (pop it up)

____ ____ ____ ____ ____ Hit ball off toe of club*

____ ____ ____ ____ ____ Hit ball off heel of club*

____ ____ ____ ____ ____ Swing club very fast and hit ball far

____ ____ ____ ____ ____ Swing club very slowly and hit ball square, straight, and not very far

____ ____ ____ ____ ____ Hit ball as perfectly as possible

– – – Face (ball curvature)

——— Path (starting direction)

Target path

Nine possible ball flight patterns
(labeled for right handed golfers):

1. straight
2. pull
3. push
4. pull hook
5. pull slice
6. straight hook
7. straight slice
8. push hook
9. push slice

Step 5 Pitching

The next basic skill in learning to play golf is pitching. The pitch shot is used when you are close to the green. For some golfers this distance is 70 yards, and for others it is 20 yards. The pitch shot differs in purpose from the full swing in that accuracy is the major goal, not distance.

WHY IS PITCHING IMPORTANT?

The pitch shot has a high trajectory with very little ball roll when it lands on the green. This makes it a desirable shot to use from near the green because it tends to stay on the green, rather than roll off. The pitch shot is a very versatile shot and can be used from about 10–90 yards from the green, depending on your skill level. This shot provides the most variation in distance of all the shots in golf.

HOW TO EXECUTE THE PITCH SHOT

The pitch shot uses the setup position and swing motion of the full swing with irons discussed in Steps 2 and 3, but with two differences: The swing length is reduced, and the stance is narrower (see Figure 5.1). The pitch shot uses a 3-to-3 or 4-to-4 swing length, rather than a 5-to-5 full swing motion. This reduced swing motion provides greater control of direction and distance. A stance that is slightly narrower than shoulder width helps you develop a swing for control, rather than distance. The clubs used for the pitch shot are the 9-iron, pitching wedge (PW), and sand wedge (SW).

Figure 5.1 Keys to Success: Pitching

(*indicates change from basic swing discussed in Step 3; see Figure 3.2)

Preparation Phase

a

Setup

1. Neutral grip
*2. Stance narrower than shoulders
3. Square foot alignment
4. Square hip alignment
5. Square shoulder alignment
6. Weight even over both feet
7. Posture with flat back, eyes over hands
8. Weight forward, mid-step to balls of feet
9. Ball position center
10. Square blade

Execution
Phase

Backswing

b

1. Arms, hands, club start as unit
2. Weight shifts to rear
3. Wrists cocked at hip level
4. Hips turn to rear
5. Back to target
*6. Backswing length 3 or 4
7. Heel of target foot off ground slightly

Forwardswing

7. Weight shifts to target side
8. Arms, hands, club move as unit
9. Wrists uncock at hip level

10. Arms, hands, club extended at contact with ball
11. Wrists recocked at target-side hip level
12. Hips turning to target

Follow-Through
Phase

c

1. Weight on target side (rear knee touches target knee)
2. Hips face target
3. Chest to target
*4. Forwardswing length 3 or 4
5. Balanced ending

Detecting Pitching Errors

The same ball flight errors that apply to the full swing apply to pitching. These should be reviewed (see Step 4). The errors listed below are the most common ones seen in pitching.

ERROR

CORRECTION

1. You hit ball on its top, giving inadequate loft in trajectory.

1. Remember that the 9-iron, PW, and SW are shortest clubs in set; you may thus be standing up too straight during execution phase. Maintain proper body posture from setup through the complete swing.

2. You hit ball too long or too short of target.

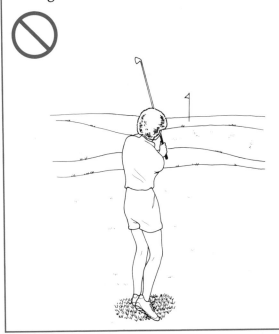

2. The club used, swing length, and swing speed determine distance of ball flight. Practice hitting balls with swing lengths of 3-to-3 and 4-to-4 (not 5-to-5) with your 9-iron, PW, and SW. Note distances ball travels.

ERROR　

CORRECTION

3. You hit ball in hosel of club.

3a. Check ball position in setup; may be too far toward your rear foot, rather than in center of stance.

　b. You may be moving body forward on forwardswing. If so, practice the One-Leg Drill from Step 3.

4. Ball flight has low trajectory.

4a. Check ball position; it may be too far back (to rear of stance) rather than in center.

　b. Practice Cocking Drill from Step 3.

5. You hit ground behind ball.

5a. Maintain posture from setup position through complete swing (see correction 3).

　b. Allow arm swing and hand action to be continuous on forwardswing through completion of swing.

Pitching Drills

1. Tee-Down Drill Without a Ball

This helps you feel the arm swing and hand action of the pitch shot. Place a tee in the hole in the end of your golf club grip. Practice taking normal swings of 3-to-3 swing length. With proper wrist cocking, the tee should point to the ground on the backswing (at position 3) and on the forwardswing (at 3).

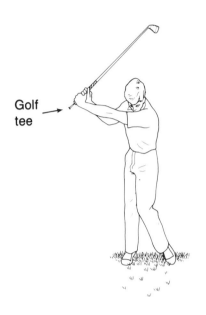

Golf tee →

Success Goal = 10 swings with correct form

Your Score = (#) _____ swings

2. Tee-Down Drill With a Ball

With a PW, SW, or 9-iron with a tee in the grip end as in the previous drill, hit balls toward targets at 20 and 40 yards. Check for tee-down position at backswing and forwardswing.

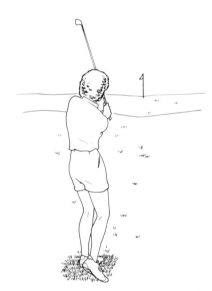

Success Goal = 100 total swings with correct form and balls landing within 15 feet of target

    a. 40 total swings with one club

        20 at 40-yard target

        20 at 20-yard target

    b. Repeat (a) with a different club

        20 at 40-yard target

        20 at 20-yard target

    c. Hit 20 shots, changing clubs and targets each time

Your Score =

a. Club used _____

   (#) _____ shots landing within 15 feet of 40-yard target (out of 20 tries)

   (#) _____ shots at 20-yard target

b. Club used _____

   (#) _____ shots landing within 15 feet of 40-yard target (out of 20)

   (#) _____ shots at 20-yard target

c. (#) _____ shots changing clubs and targets each time

3. Alternate Swing Length Drill

To determine the swing length and club you need for different distances using the pitch shot, place targets at 10-yard intervals from 40 through 90 yards. Practice hitting balls to each target using 3-to-3 and 4-to-4 swing lengths. The appropriate club and swing length for a given distance should allow you to hit balls within 10 yards of your target 50% or more of the time.

Record the average distance you hit the balls with a 3-to-3 swing length using a PW, a SW, and a 9-iron. Then switch to a 4-to-4 swing length and record the average distance hit with a PW, a SW, and a 9-iron.

Success Goal = 60 total swings

a. 3-to-3 swing length

   10 shots, PW

   10 shots, SW

   10 shots, 9-iron

b. 4-to-4 swing length

   10 shots, PW

   10 shots, SW

   10 shots, 9-iron

Your Score = distance hit

Shot	3-to-3 swing length			4-to-4 swing length		
	PW	SW	9-iron	PW	SW	9-iron
1	_____	_____	_____	_____	_____	_____
2	_____	_____	_____	_____	_____	_____
3	_____	_____	_____	_____	_____	_____
4	_____	_____	_____	_____	_____	_____
5	_____	_____	_____	_____	_____	_____
6	_____	_____	_____	_____	_____	_____
7	_____	_____	_____	_____	_____	_____
8	_____	_____	_____	_____	_____	_____
9	_____	_____	_____	_____	_____	_____
10	_____	_____	_____	_____	_____	_____
Total	_____	_____	_____	_____	_____	_____
Average	_____	_____	_____	_____	_____	_____

4. *Variable Loft Drill*

Using a single club (either a 9-iron, PW, or SW), vary the position of the ball in relation to your stance: Off the target heel, off the rear heel, and center. Note the changes in ball flight trajectory ranging from low to high, achieved without changes in your swing, but merely with changes in the positions of the teed balls.

Success Goal = 15 total swings

   5 swings, ball off the target heel

   5 swings, ball off the rear heel

   5 swings, ball in the center of stance

Your Score =

   (#) _____ swings, ball off the target heel

   (#) _____ swings, ball off the rear heel

   (#) _____ swings, ball in center of stance

Pitching
Keys to Success Checklist

You have been testing yourself by attaining each of the Success Goals for pitch shots. Next, ask your teacher, coach, or partner to evaluate your technique by using the checklist below. This pitching checklist should also be a good review of the full swing checklist you used in Step 3. *Note*: The only differences are in the *shorter swing length* and the *more narrow stance*. Items marked with an asterisk (*) vary from Step 3 list. Each item should be checked off as it is demonstrated.

Preparation Phase

Setup

_____ Grips club in neutral position (Vs in grip pointing to rear of chin)

* _____ Feet narrower than shoulder width apart

_____ Weight evenly distributed

_____ Foot alignment square to target line

_____ Hips square to target line

_____ Shoulders square to target line

_____ Posture with flat back

_____ Eyes over hands

_____ Weight forward, midstep to balls of feet

_____ Ball position center

_____ Blade of club square to target line

Execution
Phase

Backswing

_____ Arms, hands, club swing back as unit

_____ Weight shifts to rear (target knee touches rear knee)

_____ Wrists cocked at hip level

_____ Hips turn to rear (belt buckle back)

* _____ Backswing length 3 or 4

_____ Heel of target foot off ground slightly

_____ Back to target

Forwardswing

_____ Weight shifts to target side

_____ Target heel down

_____ Target knee toward target

_____ Hips return to square

_____ Arms, hands, club swing down

_____ Wrists uncocked by hip level

_____ Arms, club, hands extended at contact with ball

_____ Wrists recock at target side hip level

_____ Rear knee turned, touching target knee

_____ Hips turned to target (belt buckle turned toward target)

Follow-Through
Phase

_____ Swing continues smoothly

_____ Arms, hands, club continue until hands higher than target shoulder

_____ Hips face target

* _____ Forwardswing length 3 or 4

_____ Chest to target

_____ Hold position at end to check for balance

Step 6 Chipping

The chip shot has a low trajectory with a lot of roll when it lands on the green. This is in contrast to the pitch shot you practiced in Step 5, which has a high trajectory with little roll. The chip shot is a shorter and more controlled motion than the pitch shot. The 7- and 9-irons should be used when practicing the chip shot. After you become proficient with the 7- and 9-irons, the chip shot technique can be used with all clubs.

WHY IS CHIPPING IMPORTANT?

The purpose of the chip shot is to land the ball on the green and have it roll toward the hole. There are many situations around the green when you want to control the flight of the ball to have it land on the green and roll toward the pin. Figure 6.1 illustrates two common situations in which you use the chip shot: your previous shot lands (a) near, but not on, the green; or (b) near the green, but with sand or water between you and the green. Note that the only difference beween the two situations is that there is a sand trap present in one illustration. This sand trap (or a water hazard) should not be viewed as some insurmountable obstacle, such as a waterfall! In fact, most sand traps can be played just like any other minor obstacle.

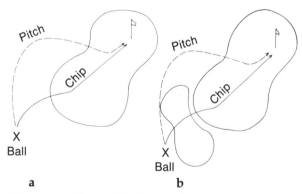

Figure 6.1 Two golf holes for chipping.

Whenever you have a choice between a pitch shot and a chip shot, you should probably choose the chip shot as long as there is room for the ball to land safely on the green and roll to the pin. The chip shot is easier to control due to the shorter swing length and less body movement it requires.

HOW TO EXECUTE THE CHIP SHOT

The swing motion of the chip shot uses only a 1-to-1 or 2-to-2 swing length, depending upon the distance required. The shoulders, arms, hands, and club move as a unit, with no wrist cock. The swinging motion is a pendular motion, which is smooth and continuous.

The setup position is important in achieving the desired low trajectory. This position differs from the pitch shot and the full swing in the following ways: Your feet are placed narrower than your shoulders, with the alignment of your feet and hips slightly open. To open your stance, move your target-side foot back about 4 inches off of the target line. This makes your body turn slightly toward the target, which helps to reduce your lower-body motion on the backswing.

Your upper and lower body lean toward the target, placing your weight more on the target side. Note that your arms and hands are just inside your target leg, which *delofts*, or decreases the natural loft of, the clubface (see Figure 6.2). Your head and swing center are on the target side of the ball. In this position you see more of the target side of the ball rather than looking straight down onto the top of the ball as in the pitch shot and full swing setups.

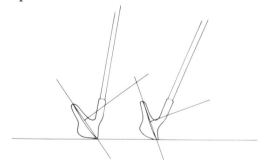

Figure 6.2 Two clubs showing natural loft and delofted.

The 7-iron and the 9-iron are suggested for the chip shot during your initial practice and play. On the golf course, your club selection for the chip shot depends on the distance the ball is from the pin and the amount of green between the ball and the pin. The amount of trajectory and roll vary between these two clubs. The 9-iron creates a higher trajectory than the 7-iron and has less roll. The rule of thumb to use as you play is to select the 9-iron for a chip shot when the distance from the ball to the pin is 10 yards or less, or there is 10 yards or less of green to the pin. Select the 7-iron for longer shots. Begin practicing with other clubs (e.g., 6, 8, PW, or SW) when, during actual play on the course, you can successfully chip the ball within 3 feet of the pin 7 out of 10 times using the 7- or 9-iron. The Keys to Success for executing the chip shot are shown in Figure 6.3.

Figure 6.3 Keys to Success:
Chipping
(* indicates change from basic full swing discussed in Step 3)

**Preparation
Phase**

Setup

a

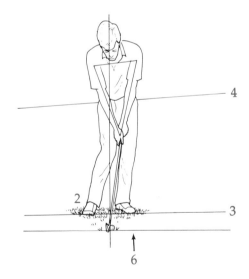

 1. Neutral grip
*2. Stance narrower than shoulders
*3. Feet-open alignment
*4. Hips-open alignment
 5. Shoulders-square alignment
*6. Weight on target side (head, swing center, hands)
 7. Posture over ball
 8. Weight forward, mid-step to balls of feet
 9. Center ball position
10. Square blade, *delofted

Execution
Phase

b   **Backswing**

1. Shoulders, arms, hands, club start as unit
*2. No weight shift
*3. No wrist cock
4. Hips turn to rear
*5. Half-turn back
*6. Backswing length 1 or 2

c   **Forwardswing**

*7. No weight shift
*8. Shoulders, arms, hands, club move as unit
*9. Maintain unitary arm action
*10. Unit at contact
*11. Hips turn halfway to target

Follow-Through
Phase

d

1. Weight on target side (rear knee touches target knee)
2. Hips face target
*3. Half-turn of chest
*4. Forwardswing length equals backswing (1 or 2)
*5. Blade square
6. Hold end position

Detecting Chipping Errors

Learning to execute a chip shot is easier if you understand how it is different from the full swing and pitch shot. Ball flight errors are the result of the swing and, therefore, are common to all swings, including the chip shot. It helps if you can see or imagine the common errors. The most common chip shot errors are listed below, along with suggestions on how to correct them.

ERROR

CORRECTION

1. Hitting the ball on its top, resulting in no loft.

1. Notice that your wrists are bent on follow-through. Instead, your hands, wrists, and arms should work as a straight unit throughout swing. Practice the Extended Club Drill (within this step). Hold follow-through to check position.

2. Ball consistently goes too far beyond target.

2a. Compare forwardswing lengths with distances ball travels.

b. Practice Ladder Drill (within this step) to develop feel for distance the ball travels.

ERROR

CORRECTION

3. You hit ground behind ball, causing ball to go too short distance.

3. Maintain proper posture with weight on target side; swing as unit throughout swing (see Figure 6.3a).

4. Chip shot with 7-iron has excessively high trajectory.

4a. Check setup position, with arms, hands, and club in straight line, with club slightly deIofted (see Figure 6.3a).

b. Maintain position by keeping hands in front of ball throughout swing.

ERROR   **CORRECTION**

5. Ball consistently goes off-target.

5a. Check setup alignment of body and club.

b. Practice Parallel Club Drill (within this step) noting target alignment and resulting shot direction.

c. Practice alignment and swing without parallel clubs.

Chipping Drills

1. Elephant Drill

The chip shot is characterized by hands that are inactive. The shoulders, arms, hands, and club work as a unit, both straight back and straight through.

Without a club, take your setup position. Let your arms hang freely. Place your palms together, creating a praying hands or elephant trunk position. Point your fingers to the rear side. Maintain extended arms while swinging them back and forth in a pendular motion (1-to-1 swing length).

Success Goal = 10 repetitions with fluid motion

Your Score = (#) _____ repetitions

2. Parallel Club Drill Without a Ball

Consistency in your alignment is important in developing a repeatable chip shot. Alignment and swing motion can be practiced together by placing two clubs on the ground, parallel to each other and apart just a little more than the width of the clubhead. Direct the clubs toward the target.

Using a 7- or 9-iron, take your setup position with your club between the parallel clubs and square to the target. Using a pendular motion, swing the club back and forth. Maintain the square blade position as you swing the club in the track.

Success Goal = 20 total swings

   a. 10 swings, 1-to-1 swing length

   b. 10 swings, 2-to-2 swing length

Your Score =

   a. (#) _____ swings, 1-to-1 swing length

   b. (#) _____ swings, 2-to-2 swing length

3. Parallel Club Drill With a Ball

Using the parallel clubs from the previous drill as a guide hit balls from between them and toward a target about 15 feet away. Alternate 1-to-1 and 2-to-2 swing lengths. Note the differences in distance and height of ball flight from varying the length of the swing. Check that every ball hit with a 2-to-2 swing length goes farther than those hit with a 1-to-1 swing length.

Success Goal = 10 total pendular swings

   a. 2 swings, 1-to-1 swing length

      2 swings, 2-to-2 swing length

   b. 2 swings, 1-to-1 swing length

      2 swings, 2-to-2 swing length

   c. 1 swing, 1-to-1 swing length

      1 swing, 2-to-2 swing length

Your Score =

   a. (#) _____ swings, 1-to-1 swing length (2)

      (#) _____ swings, 2-to-2 swing length (2)

      _____ 2-to-2 shots longer than 1-to-1

   b. (#) _____ swings, 1-to-1 swing length (2)

      (#) _____ swings, 2-to-2 swing length (2)

      _____ 2-to-2 shots longer than 1-to-1

   c. (#) _____ swing, 1-to-1 swing length (1)

      (#) _____ swing, 2-to-2 swing length (1)

      _____ 2-to-2 shot longer than 1-to-1

4. Extended Club Drill

Active hands can be the source of both distance and directional errors in the chip shot. Often your hands are active, but you may not be consciously aware of their movement. This drill helps you feel whether your hands are too active.

   Using a 9-iron, take your setup position. Add a second club as in the illustration, making an extension to your 9-iron. Take practice swings using the 1-to-1 and 2-to-2 swing lengths. If your hands are too active, the clubface will pass your hands at impact, and the second shaft will hit you in the side.

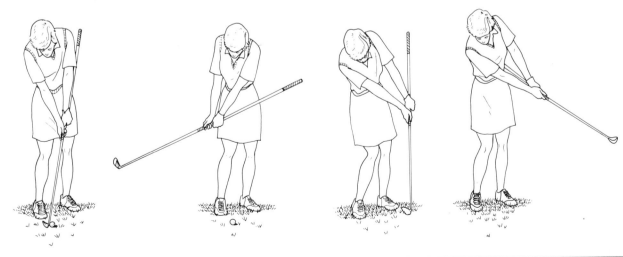

Success Goal = 20 total extended club swings

   10 swings, 1-to-1 swing length

   10 swings, 2-to-2 swing length

Your Score =

   (#) _____ swings, 1-to-1 swing length

   (#) _____ swings, 2-to-2 swing length

5. Ladder Drill

The 7- and 9-iron chip shots vary in trajectory and amount of roll. This drill helps you experiment with the amount of force required to hit balls different distances in the air.

    Place a series of clubs on the ground to serve as targets 10, 20, 30 and 40 feet away. Number the clubs from 1 (nearest) to 4. Using 1-to-1 and 2-to-2 swing lengths, practice hitting balls different distances using a single club. Then practice achieving different distances with another club. Each ball should land between the two targets you've selected as short and long boundaries for that shot.

Success Goal = 20 total shots using 7- and 9-irons

  7-iron

    2 shots, 1-to-1 swing length, landing between targets 1 and 2

    2 shots, 2-to-2 swing length, landing between targets 3 and 4

    2 shots, 1-to-1 swing length, landing between targets 2 and 3

  9-iron

    2 shots, 1-to-1 swing length, landing between targets 1 and 2

    2 shots, 2-to-2 swing length, landing between targets 3 and 4

    2 shots, 1-to-1 swing length, landing between targets 2 and 3

  7-iron

    2 shots, 1-to-1 swing length, landing between targets 2 and 3

    2 shots, 2-to-2 swing length, landing between targets 3 and 4

  9-iron

    2 shots, 1-to-1 swing length, landing between targets 2 and 3

    2 shots, 2-to-2 swing length, landing between targets 3 and 4

Your Score =

7-iron

(#) _____ shots, 1-to-1 swing length, landing between targets 1 and 2

(#) _____ shots, 2-to-2 swing length, landing between targets 3 and 4

(#) _____ shots, 1-to-1 swing length, landing between targets 2 and 3

9-iron

(#) _____ shots, 1-to-1 swing length, landing between targets 1 and 2

(#) _____ shots, 2-to-2 swing length, landing between targets 3 and 4

(#) _____ shots, 1-to-1 swing length, landing between targets 2 and 3

7-iron

(#) _____ shots, 1-to-1 swing length, landing between targets 2 and 3

(#) _____ shots, 2-to-2 swing length, landing between targets 3 and 4

9-iron

(#) _____ shots, 1-to-1 swing length, landing between targets 2 and 3

(#) _____ shots, 2-to-2 swing length, landing between targets 3 and 4

6. Obstacle Drill

The chip shot is often used on the course when a trap is between the ball and the pin (see Figure 6.1). Practicing the chip shot over obstacles helps you learn to focus on the chip motion rather than the obstacle.

Place your golf bag about 8 yards in front of your ball. Practice chipping over the bag toward targets 15, 20, and 25 yards away. Determine the appropriate club and swing length to have each ball stop within 10 feet of the desired target.

Success Goal = 20 total chips, with 10 of the balls landing within 10 feet of the desired target

3 chips 15 yards from target

3 chips 20 yards from target

3 chips 25 yards from target

2 chips 15 yards from target

2 chips 20 yards from target

2 chips 25 yards from target

1 chip 15 yards from target

1 chip 20 yards from target

1 chip 25 yards from target

1 chip 20 yards from target

1 chip 15 yards from target

Your Score =

(#) _____ chips 15 yards from target (3)

(#) _____ chips 20 yards from target (3)

(#) _____ chips 25 yards from target (3)

(#) _____ chips 15 yards from target (2)

(#) _____ chips 20 yards from target (2)

(#) _____ chips 25 yards from target (2)

(#) _____ chip 15 yards from target (1)

(#) _____ chip 20 yards from target (1)

(#) _____ chip 25 yards from target (1)

(#) _____ chip 20 yards from target (1)

(#) _____ chip 15 yards from target (1)

Chip Shot
Keys to Success Checklist

The chip shot technique can be developed quite quickly because it is shorter and more controlled than the pitch or full swing. You can become a good self-corrector as you use this checklist on yourself. Also, ask your teacher, your coach, or another trained observer to qualitatively evaluate your technique according to the checklist below. He or she may decide to create an individual practice program for you (see Appendix A). Each characteristic should be checked as it appears (* indicates change from the basic full swing technique).

Preparation Phase

Setup

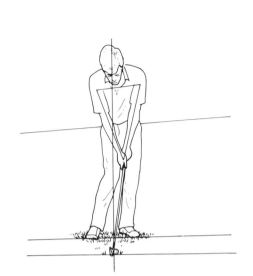

_____ Grip club in neutral position (Vs in grip pointing to rear of chin)

* _____ Feet narrower than shoulders

* _____ Feet aligned open to target

* _____ Hips aligned open to target

_____ Shoulders square to target line

* _____ Weight on target side

_____ Head to target side of ball

_____ Swing center to target side of ball

_____ Hands to target side of ball

_____ Posture with flat back

_____ Eyes over hands

_____ Weight forward midstep to balls of feet

_____ Ball position center

* _____ Blade of club square and "delofted"

Execution Phase

Backswing

* _____ Shoulders, arms, hands, club swing back as unit

* _____ No weight shift

* _____ No wrist cock

_____ Hips turn

* _____ Back to target (halfway)

* _____ Swing length 1 or 2

Forwardswing

* ____ No weight shift

* ____ Shoulders, arms, hands, club swing down as unit

* ____ Shoulders, arms, hands in same position as in setup (arms and hands in front of ball)

* ____ Hips turn halfway to target (belt buckle turned halfway toward target)

Follow-Through Phase

____ Weight on target side

____ Hips face target

* ____ Swing length equals backswing

____ Chest turned halfway to target

____ 1-to-1: hands and arms over target thigh

____ 2-to-2: hands and arms halfway between target thigh and hip

* ____ Blade square

____ Holds end position to check balance

There are two components to putting—the putting stroke and being able to read greens. The putting stroke is used primarily on the greens. It differs from the other strokes you have learned in that the ball is rolled across the grass rather than being hit into the air. This makes for greater stroke control and precision. As the ball rolls, the contour of the green affects ball direction and speed. *Reading* greens means learning to predict the influence of the green's contour on the roll of the putt.

WHY IS PUTTING IMPORTANT?

In an 18-hole round of golf, 50% of the strokes allotted toward par are for putting. This is a major indication of the role putting plays in the game. Anyone can become a good putter because strength is not a factor and, therefore, does not limit your ability. With practice you can develop a good putting stroke and begin to lower your scores while the other phases of your game are also improving.

HOW TO EXECUTE THE PUTTING STROKE AND READ GREENS

The club used in executing the putting stroke is a *putter*. The putter differs greatly from the other clubs in its design. The clubface is almost vertical, giving no loft, compared to the angled clubfaces of the other clubs. The putter is shorter than other clubs, and it has a more upright shaft.

The differences in the purpose of the stroke—to roll the ball—and the design of the club—shorter and more upright—require a modification in the setup position from other strokes. Start your putting setup position by gripping the club more in the palms of your hands rather than in the fingers (as in the full swing grip). Place the putter face behind the ball square to the desired target, with the bottom of the club flat on the ground. Assume correct posture with your eyes directly over the ball or slightly behind the ball on the target line, your arms hanging from your shoulders. Your weight should be evenly distributed across a square alignment. The ball should be positioned slightly to the target side of center.

The putting stroke motion is pendular. The club, hands, and arms work as a unit. The upper and lower body are still, but not rigid, during the stroke. The length of the back- and forwardswings are equal. The stroke length is measured in inches and varies with the length of the putt. For example, 2 to 4 inches equals a 1-to-1 putting length. The stroke is smooth and continuous, back and then through the ball (see Figure 7.1).

Figure 7.1 Keys to Success:
Putting
(* indicates difference from
basic full swing motion)

**Preparation
Phase**

a   **Setup**

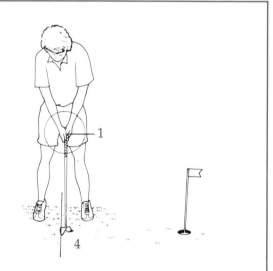

*1. Grip in palms
2. Shoulder-width stance
3. Weight even
*4. Ball target side of center
5. Square alignment of
   shoulders, hips, feet
6. Correct posture, eyes
   over ball
7. Blade square

**Execution
Phase**

Backswing

b

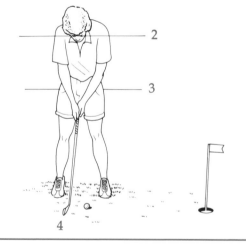

*1. Arms, hands, putter
   swing as unit
*2. Shoulders still
*3. Hips still
*4. Backswing length 1, 2,
   or 3

Forwardswing

c

*5. Arms, hands, putter
swing as unit
*6. Blade stays on target
line
*7. Upper and lower body
still

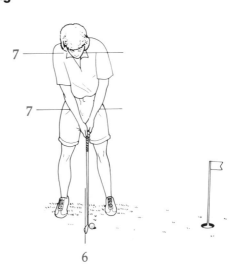

**Follow-Through
Phase**

d

*1. Arms, hands, putter
stay as unit
2. Blade square
*3. Swing length equal on
backswing and forward-
swing (1, 2, or 3)

Once you have developed a consistent putting stroke, learning to read the greens is your next objective. Greens vary in contour from very flat to very wavy. The wavy effects of a green are called *undulations* or *slopes*. A slope on the green has its greatest effect on the direction of the ball as the roll begins to slow down. With less speed (kinetic energy), the ball is less able to resist the pull of gravity, so it curves more downhill.

Imagine a clock face, as illustrated in Figure 7.2. The hole is in the middle of the face. The high point of the slope is 12 and the low point is 6; the middle points of the slope are at 3 and 9. If you putted balls from each of the points around the clock face to the hole, the lines drawn on the face illustrate the ball curvature you could expect. Note that balls putted directly uphill from 6 and directly downhill from 12 are relatively straight. From each of the other points, as the ball slows down, it curves down the slope.

To apply the clock analogy to reading greens, move to a position about 10 feet directly behind your ball in line with the hole. Bend down or kneel (see Figure 7.3) in order to effectively see the slope of the green, specifically the slope closest to the hole. If there are no slopes, align the blade directly with the middle of the hole for a straight putt. If there is a slope, determine the high and the low points of the slope (i.e., 12 and 6 on the clock face) and where your ball is relative to those points. Visualize the ball rolling up or down the slope and curving into the hole. Pick a spot a few inches on the high side of the hole. Align your blade to that spot. As the ball rolls to the spot and slows down, it will curve toward the hole.

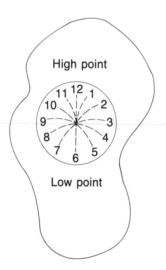

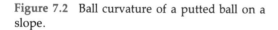

Figure 7.2   Ball curvature of a putted ball on a slope.

Figure 7.3   Bend down in order to see the slope of the green.

Detecting Putting Errors

Errors in putting are similar to those in the full swing and can be detected by watching the roll of the ball. The errors listed below are the most common ones in putting.

ERROR

CORRECTION

1. On straight putts, ball consistently rolls to side of hole.

1a. Check your setup position: Square clubface and body alignment.

 b. Use clubs on the ground for direction; practice putting stroke using Track Drill (within this step).

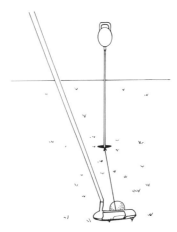

2. Putts land too far past the hole.

2a. Maintain a firm, unitary swing of arms, hands, and putter through the ball, rather than using wrists.

 b. Practice Cluster Putting Drill (within this step).

ERROR

CORRECTION

3. Putts come up short of hole.

3. Make backswing and forwardswing equal.

4. On downhill putts, ball consistently misses to left of the hole (for right-handed putter).

4a. You aim putts off-line. Check setup position for eyes directly over ball and alignment (use Eye Drill within this step).

  b. Practice green reading using the Green Clock Drill in this Step.

ERROR | **CORRECTION**

5. Putts have inconsistent distance and direction.

5. Check setup position.

Putting Drills

1. Arm Swing Drill

The precision of the putting stroke is enhanced by the compactness of the unitary swing and your posture with your eyes over the ball.

a. Without a putter or ball, take your posture position. Bend your arms at the elbows and place your palms together. Swing your arms and hands back and forth as a unit without moving your shoulders. Use a 1-to-1 swing length.

b. Repeat (a) with a putter. When you add the putter, it becomes part of the unitary swing. The grip pressure is firm, but not tight, to prevent the hands from moving.

Success Goal = 20 total swings

  a. 10 swings without putter

  b. 10 swings with putter

Your Score =

  a. (#) _____ swings without putter

  b. (#) _____ swing with putter

2. Eye Drill

The position of your eyes over the ball or target line increases your ability to control the path of the club. You can check your eye position in the following way: With a club and ball, take your setup over the ball. Hold your putter in your dominant hand and an extra ball in your target hand. Move the putter from behind the ball on the ground and drop the extra ball from the bridge of your nose. The ball should fall on top of, or slightly behind, the other ball, but still on the target line.

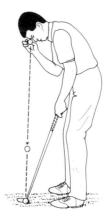

Success Goal = 10 repetitions with correct form, dropped ball landing on other ball or target line 7 of 10 times

Your Score = (#) _____ times out of 10 that dropped ball lands as desired

3. Track Drill

Developing a consistent path improves your directional control.

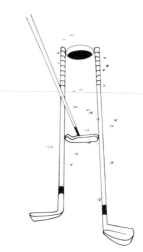

a. Place two clubs on the ground parallel to the target line and just farther apart than your putter blade. Practice swinging the putter between the clubs, using a pendulum motion and maintaining a square blade as it moves back and forth.

Success Goal = 20 putting strokes without hitting either of parallel clubs

Your Score = (#) _____ putting strokes

b. With the ends of the clubs next to a hole, practice putting into the hole. Begin from about 1 foot away from the hole and gradually move back to 3 feet away.

Success Goal = 30 consecutive total putts made

10 putts from 1 foot

10 putts from 2 feet

10 putts from 3 feet

Your Score =

(#) _____ consecutive putts from 1 foot

(#) _____ consecutive putts from 2 feet

(#) _____ consecutive putts from 3 feet

c. Remove the tracks and practice putting balls, starting at 1 foot from the hole and moving back to 6 feet.

Success Goal = 60 total putts from 1-6 feet away from hole

10 putts from 1 foot

10 putts from 2 feet

10 putts from 3 feet

10 putts from 4 feet

10 putts from 5 feet

10 putts from 6 feet

Your Score =

(#) _____ putts from 1 foot

(#) _____ putts from 2 feet

(#) _____ putts from 3 feet

(#) _____ putts from 4 feet

(#) _____ putts from 5 feet

(#) _____ putts from 6 feet

4. Tape Drill

Learning to control the swing length of your stroke is important in developing consistent distance control. Place a 12-inch piece of tape on the floor, carpet, or green. Make a perpendicular mark across the tape in its center (at 6 inches). On either side of the mark, measure and mark 2, 4, and 6 inches away from the center. Label the marks *1, 2, 3,* going away from the center in both directions.

a. Practice putting without a ball, moving the blade with tape swing lengths (not standard swing lengths) of 1-to-1, 2-to-2, and 3-to-3. Hold each finish to check for a square blade.

Success Goal = 15 total strokes

   5 strokes, 1-to-1 swing length

   5 strokes, 2-to-2 swing length

   5 strokes, 3-to-3 swing length

Your Score =

   (#) _____ strokes, 1-to-1 swing length

   (#) _____ strokes, 2-to-2 swing length

   (#) _____ strokes, 3-to-3 swing length

b. Practice putting balls from the tape. Before each putt, take one practice stroke away from the ball the same swing length you will use to hit the ball. Then step up to the ball and actually stroke it, using the same swing length as the practice stroke.

Success Goal = 15 total putts, using practice stroke before each

   5 putts, 1-to-1 swing length

   5 putts, 2-to-2 swing length

   5 putts, 3-to-3 swing length

Your Score =

   (#) _____ putts, 1-to-1 swing length

   (#) _____ putts, 2-to-2 swing length

   (#) _____ putts, 3-to-3 swing length

5. *Putting Ladder Drill*

Practice your stroke, checking for a square blade at finish and noting the distances the ball goes with each swing length.

Place 5 clubs in a ladder formation. The first club should be 10 feet away, with the other clubs at 3-foot intervals (10, 13, 16, 19, and 22 feet). Practice putting for distance; don't worry about aiming at a specific target or hole. For example, decide to putt a ball between the second and third clubs (rungs) on the ladder.

Success Goal = putting 15 total balls, attempting to make the balls quit rolling between the desired club distances

3 putts at 10 feet

3 putts at 13 feet

3 putts at 16 feet

3 putts at 19 feet

3 putts at 22 feet

Your Score =

(#) _____ putts at 10 feet

(#) _____ putts at 13 feet

(#) _____ putts at 16 feet

(#) _____ putts at 19 feet

(#) _____ putts at 22 feet

6. *Cluster Putting Drill*

Judging distance when putting depends on having a stroke that can be repeated. Your ability to feel the stroke can be improved through practice on this drill.

Take 3 balls. Without watching its roll, putt the first ball far enough so that it lands outside your peripheral vision. Still without looking, putt the next 2 balls, trying to have the balls come to rest in a cluster, nudging each other. For every group of 3 putts, try to cluster second and third putts around first. Focus on developing the feel of a repeating stroke.

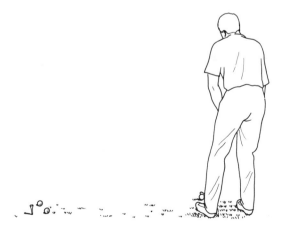

Success Goal = 15 total putts, focusing on developing a feel for the repeated stroke and hitting the first ball in each group of 3 to a new distance

3 putts at location A (1st ball)

3 putts to location B (4th ball)

3 putts to location C (7th ball)

3 putts to location D (10th ball)

3 putts to location E (13th ball)

Your Score =

(#) _____ putts to location A

(#) _____ putts to location B

(#) _____ putts to location C

(#) _____ putts to location D

(#) _____ putts to location E

7. Line Drill

To practice short putts and controlling the length of your putting backswing, place 6 balls 3 inches apart on the target line to the hole. Starting with the ball closest to the hole, putt the balls into the hole. When a putt is missed, start again with all 6 balls.

Success Goal = 5 repetitions of making 6 consecutive putts

Your Score =

(#) _____ made out of 6 putts

(#) _____ made out of 6 putts

(#) _____ made out of 6 putts

(#) _____ made out of 6 putts

(#) _____ made out of 6 putts

8. Green Clock Drill

Through systematic practice of watching balls roll on a green with various degrees of slope, you begin to be able to predict putt curvature. Once you start predicting ball roll, compare what you thought would happen with what actually occurs.

Place 12 balls 5 feet away from the hole in a circle, spacing balls like numerals on a clock face. Start putting at the lowest point on the slope (6 o'clock). Read the green and go through your entire setup procedure with each putt. Continue to putt in a counterclockwise direction (i.e., 5, 4, 3, and so on). Take careful note of the roll of each ball.

Success Goal = 12 total putts, charting the curvature of each putt by drawing dotted lines on the clock face

Your Score = interpreting your putting chart

(#) _____ putts going in hole

(#) _____ putts coming up short of hole

(#) _____ putts going beyond hole (too long)

(#) _____ putts missing hole to right

(#) _____ putts missing hole to left

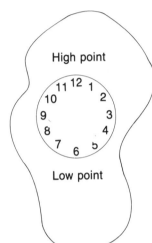

Putting
Keys to Success Checklist

You have been quantitatively testing yourself by attaining each of the Step 7 Success Goals. Next, ask your teacher, your coach, or another trained observer to qualitatively evaluate your technique according to the checklist below by checking each item as it is demonstrated (* indicates difference from full swing).

Preparation Phase

Setup

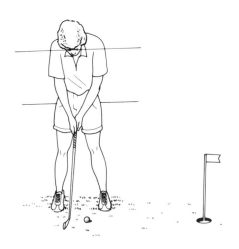

_____ Reads green

_____ Selects target

* _____ Grip in palms
(Vs in grip point toward respective shoulders)

_____ Feet shoulder width apart

_____ Weight evenly distributed

_____ Feet alignment square to target line

_____ Hips square to target line

_____ Shoulders square to target line

_____ Posture with flat back

_____ Eyes over the ball

_____ Weight forward, midstep to balls of feet

* _____ Ball position target side of center

_____ Blade of club square to target line

Execution Phase

Backswing

* _____ Arms, hands, putter swing back as unit

* _____ Arms bent at elbows

* _____ No weight shift

* _____ No wrist cock

* _____ Hips still

* _____ Shoulders still

* _____ Swing length 1, 2, or 3

Forwardswing

* _____ No weight shift

* _____ Arms, hands, putter start as unit

* _____ No wrist movement

* _____ Arms, hands, putter as unit at contact with ball

* _____ Shoulders still

* _____ Hips still

* _____ Blade stays on target line

Follow-Through Phase

_____ Swing continues smoothly

* _____ Arms, hands, putter continue as unit

* _____ Hips same position as setup

* _____ Swing length 1, 2, or 3

* _____ Shoulders same as setup

_____ Holds position at end to check for balance

_____ Square blade at end

_____ Holds for a moment to check squareness

_____ Swing length equal on both sides (length of follow-through = length of backswing)

Step 8 Sand Shots

The two shots presented in this step—the explosion shot and the buried lie shot—are used in hitting from sand traps or bunkers around the green. Sand shots create a different challenge to golfers than the shots you have been practicing in Steps 3 through 7. The soft texture of sand creates three conditions that you have not met in the previous steps: (a) the lie—the ball either resting on top of the sand or buried below the surface of the sand (see Figure 8.1); (b) a stance stability concern not found when hitting from grass (the fairway or rough areas); and (c) the club not contacting the ball directly, but instead contacting the sand, which pushes the ball out of the trap. In this step you learn how to utilize your full swing motion effectively by modifying your setup. This lets you accommodate the three sand conditions in executing the two sand shots, the explosion shot and the buried lie shot.

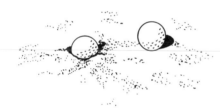

Figure 8.1 Ball buried (left) and ball on top of sand.

WHY ARE SAND SHOTS IMPORTANT?

Sand traps are strategically placed on courses in the landing areas where the majority of players hit their tee shots and around the greens. The frequency of your use of sand shots depends on the course or courses you play. The number of sand traps on a given course can range from none to 100 or more.

Your ability to hit consistently out of traps helps you develop confidence and save strokes during a round of golf. For many players, the sight of a sand trap causes a panic button to go off. This doesn't need to happen to you. The sand shots are two of the easiest shots in golf because you don't hit the ball—you hit the sand, and the ball flies out with the sand.

When your ball lands in a sand trap, the generally soft texture of the sand creates a hitting surface and ball lie that are different from those found on the fairway or with the grass conditions on which you have thus far practiced. The sand also adds the challenges of your maintaining your balance during the swing and adapting to the rules that prohibit you from letting your club touch the sand before your forwardswing.

Your understanding of the modifications needed in the setup position and the use of the sand wedge to allow for the different sand textures can help you become an overall better golfer.

HOW TO EXECUTE THE SAND SHOTS

The *sand wedge* is the club specifically designed for use in the sand trap. This club differs from other irons in that it is slightly heavier and that the sole, or bottom, of the club is wider and angles down lower than the front edge of the club (see Figure 8.2). The differences in club design make it easier to swing through the sand. The texture of the sand, though soft, is heavier than grass and offers greater resistance when contacted during the swing.

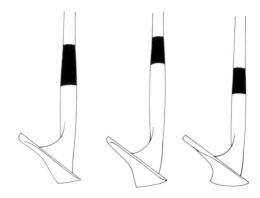

Figure 8.2 Types of sand wedges.

There are two basic sand shots: The explosion shot and the buried lie shot; the lie of the ball in the sand determines which one is selected. When the ball rests on top of the sand, more similar to a ball in the fairway, the explosion shot is used. The buried lie shot is used, as the name implies, when the ball is partially buried or rests completely below the level of the sand. Each shot is now discussed separately, with special note of the specific modifications in the setup positions from that of the full swing.

Explosion Shot

The explosion shot is similar to an iron shot from the fairway. There are three setup modifications from the full swing affecting clubface alignment, body alignment, and stance. The clubface is slightly open for the explosion shot to avoid digging into the sand too deeply. Before gripping the club, open the clubface slightly; then take your neutral grip position.

Your body alignment should be slightly open, rather than square as in the full swing. This adjustment counteracts the influence of the open clubface (Step 4), producing a straight shot rather than a push.

The stance modification provides you greater stability during the swing. As you take your stance, dig your toes into the sand a few inches. This places more weight toward the balls of your feet. By placing your feet below the level of the sand, the club enters the sand several inches to the rear side of the ball position.

These setup modifications allow you to use your full swing motion in the sand. The trajectory of the explosion shot is fairly high, and the ball lands with little roll. The sand wedge (SW) by design is the most effective club for the explosion shot. However, a pitching wedge (PW) or 9-iron can also be used. Directional and distance control come with practice and experience (see Figure 8.3).

Figure 8.3 *Keys to Success: Explosion Sand Shot*
(* indicates difference from basic full swing motion)

Preparation Phase

a

Setup

1. Neutral grip
2. Feet shoulder width
*3. Open foot alignment
*4. Open hip alignment
*5. Open shoulder alignment
6. Weight even over both feet
7. Posture over ball
*8. Weight forward, toes dig into sand
9. Ball position center to target side of center
*10. Blade open

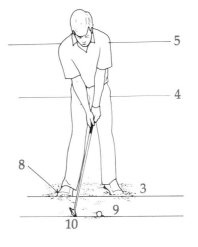

**Execution
Phase**

Backswing

b

1. Arms, hands, club start as unit
2. Weight shifts to rear (target knee touches rear knee)
3. Wrists cocked at hip level
4. Hips turn to rear
5. Back to target
*6. Backswing length 4 or 5

Explosion Sand Shot

Forwardswing

c

7. Weight shifts to target side
8. Arms, hands, club start down as unit
9. Wrists uncocked at hip level
10. Arms, hands, club extended at ball contact
11. Wrists recock at target-side hip level
12. Hips turned to target

Explosion Sand Shot

**Follow-Through
Phase**

d

1. Weight on target side (rear knee touches target knee)
2. Hips face target
3. Chest to target
4. Forwardswing length 4 or 5
5. Balanced ending

Explosion Sand Shot

Buried Lie Sand Shot

The buried lie shot differs in the setup position from the explosion shot and the full swing because the club must either swing down more steeply or dig into the sand to pop the ball out from the buried lie. The setup position is similar to the chip shot, but using a full swing motion. There are five setup modifications from the full swing, in stance, body alignment, weight distribution, clubface alignment, and ball position (see Figure 8.4).

Your stance here is the same as in the explosion shot, with your toes dug several inches into the sand for stability. With this position, as indicated with the explosion shot, the club enters the sand to the rear side of center. Your body alignment is slightly open for your feet and hips, while your shoulders are square to the target line. Your weight distribution is to the target side, with the upper and lower body leaning toward the target. This is the same position as in the chip shot.

The clubface position is square, but delofted because the ball position is to the rear side of center, just forward of the point where the club enters the sand.

The modifications in this setup position for the buried lie shot produce a shot with a low trajectory and a lot of roll. A sand wedge, pitching wedge, or 9-iron are effective. A higher trajectory is possible with the sand wedge, which should be used whenever possible for the buried lie shot.

Figure 8.4 Keys to Success:
Buried Lie Shot

(* indicates difference from
regular full swing keys)

Preparation Phase

Setup

a

1. Neutral grip
2. Feet shoulder width
*3. Open foot alignment
*4. Open hip alignment
5. Square shoulder
   alignment
*6. Weight on target side
   (head, hands)
7. Posture over ball
*8. Weight forward, toes
   dug into sand
*9. Ball position rear side
   of center
*10. Square blade (delofted)

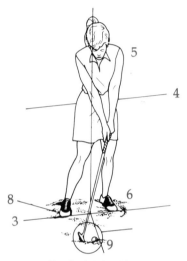

Buried Lie Shot

Execution Phase

Backswing

b

1. Arms, hands, club start
   as unit
2. Weight shifts to rear
   (target knee touches
   rear knee)
3. Wrists cocked at hip
   level
4. Hips turn to rear
5. Back to target
*6. Backswing length 4

Buried Lie Shot

Forwardswing

7. Weight shifts to target side

8. Arms, hands, club start down as unit

9. Wrists uncocked at hip level

10. Arms, hands, club extended at ball contact

11. Wrists recock at target-side hip level

12. Hips turned to target

Follow-Through
Phase

c

1. Weight on target side (rear knee touches target knee)

2. Hips face target

3. Chest to target

*4. Forwardswing length 4

5. Balanced ending

Buried Lie Shot

Detecting Sand Shot Errors

Sand shots can be analyzed by looking at two different situations: Explosion Shots and Buried Lie Shots. In order to detect problems with these shots, it is important to differentiate between them. The explosion shot is similar to an iron shot from the fairway, while the buried lie shot is different from the full swing motion because the club must swing down more steeply in order to dig into the sand to pop up the ball. The errors listed below are the most common problems from the sand.

ERROR

CORRECTION

1. Your swing takes too much sand, and the ball does not come out of the trap consistently.

1a. Check ball position; practice.

 b. Practice Sandy Line Drills, noting consistent contact point.

 c. Position ball in stance 1 inch to target side of point where you contact sand.

 d. Maintain arm swing.

2. You hit the ball, not the sand behind the ball.

2a. Check setup and ball position.

 b. Practice Sandy Line Drills; focus on a line (1–2 inches) behind ball in contacting sand.

ERROR

CORRECTION

3. Shots fly out of sand and go too far, even though sand seems to be properly displaced.

3a. Check setup position; move ball position slightly forward in your stance to take more sand.

  b. Check posture, put weight more forward with *toes dug in*.

  c. Practice the Bunker Distance Drill.

4. Ball scoots off in direction of a push, having been hit by hosel.

4. Check setup position, alignment, and ball postion; alignment may be too open and ball position too far to the rear.

Sand Shot Drills

1. Sandy Line Drill: Explosion Shot

The key to sand shots is to contact the sand in the same point in your swing each time. This helps you develop confidence in swinging *through* the sand, making the ball fly out with the sand. Practice the Sandy Line Drill to aid in developing this feel and consistency.

a. Draw a line in the sand and take your setup position for the explosion shot. Place the line in the center of your stance. Make practice swings without balls, moving up the line after each swing. Note where you contact the sand in relation to the line. Be sure to practice your entire setup procedure prior to each swing.

b. Draw a new line where you were consistently hitting the sand in part (a). Place 5 balls 1 inch in front (target side) of the new line. Be sure each ball is resting on top of the sand. Practice hitting through the line and watching the balls fly out of the sand. Do not worry about the direction or distance of your shots. Remember, your *first* objective is to get out of the sand.

Success Goal = 15 total swings with correct form

   a. 10 swings without balls, hitting the sand at a consistent location relative to the line

   b. 5 swings at line, continuing through balls placed 1 inch to target side of line

Your Score =

   a. (#) _____ swings at line only (10)

   b. (#) _____ swings at balls (5)

2. Sandy Line Drill: Buried Lie Shot

a. Draw a line in the sand (see previous drill) and take your setup position for a buried lie. Place the line in the center of your stance. Be sure to review the Keys to Success, noting the differences in the setup for the explosion shot versus the buried lie shot. Taking practice swings now, note where you contact the sand in relation to the line.

b. Draw a new line at the point where you consistently hit the sand in part (a). Now slightly bury 5 balls *on* the line drawn in the sand (note that this buried lie drill has the balls on the line, whereas the explosion shot drill had the balls 1 inch to the target side of the line). Be sure the balls are slightly buried in the sand. Practice hitting through the line and watching the balls fly out of the sand. Do not worry about the direction or the distance of your shots. Remember, your first objective is to get out of the sand.

Success Goal = 15 total swings with the correct form

    a. 10 swings without balls, at consistent location relative to line

    b. 5 swings, balls buried on the new line

Your Score =

    a. (#) _____ swings at consistent location (10)

    b. (#) _____ swings at balls (5)

3. Fried Egg Visual Image Drill for Explosion Sand Shot

Some golfers like to imagine that a golf ball sitting in the sand is like a fried egg. You want to imagine putting the spatula under the yolk of the egg without breaking the yellow.

Draw an oval in the sand. Imagine that a golf ball in its center is the yolk of an egg. Take your stance with the entire "egg" in the center of your stance. Hit the ball out, thinking about the club as a spatula scraping the egg off the bottom of the frying pan, scraping under the yolk so as not to break it. Draw 5 of these ovals in the sand and place a ball in the center of each.

Success Goal = hitting each "egg" out of the sand

Your Score = (#) _____ "eggs" hit

4. Overlapping Grip Sand Drill: Explosion Shot

One common tendency in hitting sand shots is for the arms to decelerate because the target arm slows down. To feel the target arm throughout the swing, practice this drill.

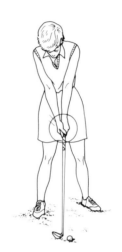

a. Take your setup position for the explosion shot. Grip the club with your target hand, then place your rear hand on top of your target hand. Practice swinging the club 10 times, knocking sand out of the trap using the line drill used in the Sandy Line Drill: Explosion Shot.

b. Draw a new line at the point where you consistently hit the sand in part (a). Place 5 balls 1 inch toward the target side of the new line. Hit the sand and balls out of the bunker.

Success Goal = 15 total swings with correct form

   10 swings hitting sand in same spot 7 of 10 times

   5 swings hitting sandy line and continuing through balls

Your Score =

   (#) _____ swings in the same spot (10)

   (#) _____ swings hitting the sandy line and balls (5)

5. Overlapping Grip Sand Drill: Buried Lie Shot

Take your setup position for the buried lie shot. Place a line in the center of your stance. Grip the club with your target hand, then place your rear hand on top of your target hand as in the previous drill.

a. Take 10 swings without balls in the setup position for the buried lie shot. Note where the club strikes the sand on each swing.

b. Draw a new line in the sand at the point where you consistently hit the sand in part (a). Now slightly bury 5 balls *on* the line drawn in the sand. Be sure each ball is slightly buried. Practice hitting the line and the ball out of the sand while using the overlapping grip. Focus your attention on feeling your target arm continue to swing throughout the swing.

Success Goal = 15 total swings with proper setup

10 swings hitting sand at consistent location relative to line

5 swings at balls slightly buried on target line

Your Score =

a. (#) _____ swings hitting the sand at consistent location (10)
b. (#) _____ swings at balls slighty buried (5)

6. Bunker Distance Drill

Distance control in the sand can be practiced in the same ways as pitching, chipping, and putting. Establish four targets 5, 10, 20, and 30 yards away. Practice adjusting your swing length or speed to produce a sand shot that flies to each of those target distances.

a. Using an explosion shot, hit 3 balls to each target

b. Using a buried lie shot, hit 3 balls to each target.

Success Goal = hitting 24 total shots, 3 for each distance and type of shot

  a. Explosion Shot

     3 balls hit at 5-yard target

     3 balls hit at 10-yard target

     3 balls hit at 20-yard target

     3 balls hit at 30-yard target

  b. Repeat goal (a) using the buried lie sand shot.

Your Score =

a. Explosion Shot

(#) _____ balls hit at 5-yard target

(#) _____ balls hit at 10-yard target

(#) _____ balls hit at 20-yard target

(#) _____ balls hit at 30-yard target

b. Buried Lie Shot

(#) _____ balls hit at 5-yard target

(#) _____ balls hit at 10-yard target

(#) _____ balls hit at 20-yard target

(#) _____ balls hit at 30-yard target

Sand Shots
Keys to Success Checklist

Executing sand shots is not difficult if you (a) *assess* the lie of the ball as resting either on sand or below the sand; (b) *select* the appropriate shot for the lie (the explosion shot for those on top of the sand and the buried lie shot for those below the surface of the sand); and (c) *modify* your setup position according to the type of shot needed. The following checklist can help you become more comfortable with the differences in the two shots. Remember the key idea with both sand shots is to swing *through* the sand. Asterisks denote the differences in the sand shot from the full swing motion. Have a partner, teacher, or coach check off each characteristic as you demonstrate it.

Preparation Phase

Setup

Explosion Shot	Buried Lie Shot	
____	____	Grips club in neutral position (Vs in grip pointing rear of chin)
____		Feet shoulder width apart
		Weight distribution:
____		Evenly distributed
	* ____	Target side
		Foot alignment to target line:
* ____	* ____	Open
		Hips to target line:
* ____	* ____	Open
		Shoulders to target line:
	____	Square
* ____		Open
____	____	Posture with flat back
____	____	Eyes over hands
* ____	* ____	Weight forward, toes dug into sand
		Ball position:
* ____		Center to target side of center
	* ____	Rear side of center
		Blade of club:
* ____		Open
	____	Square (delofted)

Explosion Sand Shot

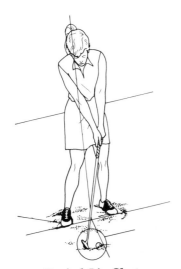

Buried Lie Shot

Execution Phase

Backswing

Explosion Sand Shot **Buried Lie Shot**

Explosion Shot	*Buried Lie Shot*	
___	___	Arms, hands, club swing back as unit
___	___	Weight shifts to rear (target knee touches rear knee)
___	___	Wrists cocked at hip level
___	___	Hips turn to rear (belt buckle back)
		Backswing length:
	* ___	4
* ___		4 or 5
	___	Heel of target foot off ground slightly
		Hands over rear shoulder in full turn
___		Club parallel to ground

Forwardswing

Both Explosion Sand Shot and Buried Lie Shot

Explosion Shot	*Buried Lie Shot*	
___	___	Weight shift to target side:
___	___	Target heel down
___	___	Target knee toward target
___	___	Hips return to square
___	___	Arms, hands, club swing down as unit
___	___	Wrists uncocked at hip level
___	___	Arms, club, hands extended at contact with ball
	___	Wrists recock at target-side hip level
___	___	Hips turned to target (belt buckle turned toward target)

Follow-Through
Phase

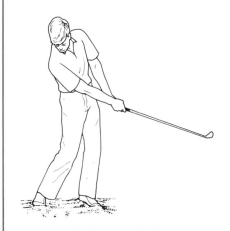

Explosion Sand Shot

Buried Lie Shot

Explosion Shot	*Buried Lie Shot*	
_____	_____	Swing continues smoothly
_____	_____	Hips face target
		Forwardswing length:
* _____		4 or 5
	* _____	4
_____	_____	Chest to target
_____	_____	Holds position at end to check for balance

Step 9   **Uneven Lies**

One of the distinguishing features of a golf course is the type of terrain on which it is built. This varies from one geographical area to another as well as within the design of the course itself. For example, the courses in Florida tend to be very flat, whereas those in Vermont are very hilly. Playing on different types of terrain creates a challenge to golfers.

In the previous steps, you have been practicing on relatively flat terrain, similar to Florida's, in which the ball and your feet have been on the same level. When you practice or play courses in mountainous areas or where there are hills or slopes, there are times when the ball and your feet are on different levels. These situations are called *uneven lies* and require modifications in your setup position.

Two types of uneven lies are presented in this step: *sidehill lies* and *uphill/downhill lies*. When the golf ball comes to rest in a nice, flat, grassy area, it is referred to as a *good lie*. Balls that land on up- or downhill lies and sidehill lies are therefore sometimes referred to as *trouble shots*. In fact, though, they are ''trouble'' only if you do not practice them and

understand the effects of these lies on your setup and on the action of the ball.

WHY ARE UNEVEN LIES IMPORTANT?

Not all golf courses are flat. Knowledge of how to adjust the setup position for the various lies helps to reduce the anxiety of playing on hills. Unfortunately, not all practice areas have hills or slopes on which to practice these types of shots. However, with just a basic understanding of how to play the shots, you will find that you can quickly adapt to uneven terrains.

HOW TO EXECUTE UNEVEN LIES

Again, there are two types of uneven lies: sidehill and uphill/downhill lies. The location of the ball relative to your feet distinguishes the two types of lies. In sidehill lies, the ball is either above or below your feet (see Figures 9.1a and b); in the uphill and downhill lies, the ball is even with your feet (see Figures 9.1c and d).

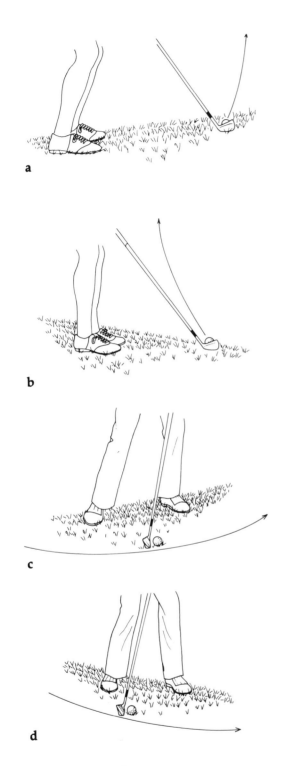

Figure 9.1 Sidehill lies (a, b); uphill lie (c); downhill lie (d).

The full swing motion you learned in Step 3, using the swing lengths of 5-to-5 or 4-to-4, is appropriate for most uneven lies. The swing length is determined by the degree of slope and the distance to the desired target area. The more severe the slope, the greater the demand for balance and control, which limits your swing length and potential distance achieved.

The major difference in the uneven and the regular fairway shots is in the setup position modifications due to the terrain. The sidehill lies and the uphill and downhill lies are now discussed separately, with specific note given their differences in setup.

Sidehill Lies

Sidehill lies have the ball either above or below your feet when you take your stance. These lies differ slightly in the setup position from your regular full swing with an iron. Both sidehill lies require adjustment to an intermediate target rather than directly on the primary target, because the natural ball flight from sidehill lies tends to curve in the downward direction of the slope. If the ball is above your feet, it tends to hook; if below your feet, it tends to slice. As you take your setup position, select an intermediate target about 10 yards to the right or left of the desired target, depending on the lie.

If the ball position is above (higher than) your feet, it requires one additional setup modification. Because the hill is closer to your hands as you set up, grip the club about 3 inches from the top; then execute your regular swing. This "choke-up" grip should be adjusted based on the degree of slope.

When the ball is positioned below your feet, it tends to impair your balance during the swing. To enhance your balance, place more weight toward your heels, rather than on the midstep to the balls of your feet as in your regular swing (see Figure 9.2).

Figure 9.2   Keys to Success:
Sidehill Lies
(* indicates difference from
basic full swing motion)

Preparation
Phase

Setup

*1. Neutral grip
  • Ball below: full length
  • Ball above: choke up
2. Feet shoulder width
3. Square foot alignment
4. Square hip alignment
5. Square shoulder align-
  ment
6. Weight even over both
  feet
7. Posture over ball
*8. Weight distribution
  • Ball below: toward
  heels
  • Ball above: even
9. Ball position center to
  target side of center
10. Square blade

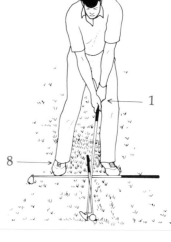

a   Ball above feet   b   Ball below feet

Execution
Phase
(see Figures 3.2c-h)

Backswing

1. Arms, hands, club start
  as unit
2. Weight shifts to rear
3. Wrists cocked at hip
  level

4. Hips turn to rear
5. Back to target
6. Backswing length 4 or 5

Forwardswing

7. Weight shifts to target side
8. Arms, hands, club start down as unit
9. Wrists uncock at hip level

10. Arms, hands, club extended at contact
11. Wrists recocked at hip level
12. Hips turned to target

Follow-Through Phase
(see Figures 3.2i-k)

1. Weight on target side
2. Hips face target
3. Chest to target

4. Forwardswing length 4 or 5
5. Balanced ending

Uphill and Downhill Lies

In uphill and downhill lies, the ball is even with your feet in your stance—the only thing is, your feet are at different levels on a slope. In an uphill lie, your forwardswing must go up the slope (i.e., to the top of the slope); in a downhill lie, your forwardswing must go down the slope (i.e., to the bottom of the slope).

These lies require four modifications of your full swing setup positions. The alignment requires an intermediate target, as with the sidehill lie (previously discussed), because the slope affects the ball flight. Uphill lie shots tend to hook; downhill lie shots tend to slice.

Grip the club in a choked-up position about 3 inches from the top. This choked-up position is necessary because your hands are closer to the slope on both lies. The ball position is closer to the level of the high foot on the slope. Move away from the ball and take several practice swings. Note where the club contacts the ground. This is your ball position. The practice swings also help you determine the amount of choking up required. Position your shoulders parallel to the slope. This makes it easier to swing the club with the slope (see Figure 9.3).

Figure 9.3 Keys to Success: Uphill and Downhill Lies

(* indicates difference from the basic full swing setup discussed in Step 3)

Preparation Phase

Setup

*1. Neutral grip, choked up

2. Feet shoulder width

*3. Alignment to intermediate target

4. Square foot alignment

*5. Square shoulder alignment parallel to slope

*6. Weight even over both feet (lean into hill)

7. Posture over ball

8. Weight forward, mid-step to balls of feet

*9. Ball position toward high foot

*10. Blade square to intermediate target line

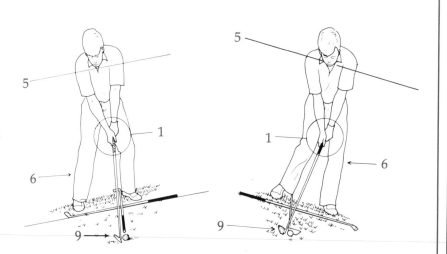

a. Uphill Lie   **b. Downhill Lie**

Execution Phase
(see Figures 3.2c-h)

Backswing

1. Arms, hands, club start as unit

2. Weight shifts to rear (target knee touches rear knee)

3. Wrists cocked at hip level

4. Hips turn to rear

5. Back to target

6. Backswing length 4 or 5

Forwardswing

7. Weight shifts to target side
8. Arms, hands, club start down as unit
9. Wrists uncocked at hip level

10. Arms, hands, club extended at contact
11. Wrists recocked at hip level
12. Hips turned to target

**Follow-Through
Phase
(see Figures 3.2i-k)**

1. Weight on target side (rear knee touches target knee)
2. Hips face target

3. Chest to target
4. Swing length 4 or 5
5. Balanced ending

Detecting Uneven Lie Shot Errors

Learning to execute golf shots from various types of slopes is easier if you understand how these shots are different from flat shots and if you can see or imagine the common errors. The setups differ from the basic full swing setup. Once you are familiar with these, you will have no problem adjusting to slopes.

The most common problems with hitting from sloping surfaces are listed below, along with suggestions on how to correct them. Remember, the swing motion for uneven lies is the same as the full swing motion (see Step 3 for additional ball flight errors).

ERROR   **CORRECTION**

Uphill/Downhill Lie

1. You top ball on downhill lies.

1. Maintain good posture throughout swing.

2. You hit downhill shots "fat" (stubbing club into ground).

2a. Position shoulders parallel to slope (see Figure 9.3b).

  b. Position ball toward high foot.

3. You consistently pull uphill shots with wood.

3a. Check setup alignment.

  b. Uphill lies tend to hook, so be sure to use intermediate target (see Figure 9.3a).

ERROR   **CORRECTION**

Sidehill Lie

4. You hit sidehill shots "fat" (stubbing club into ground) when the ball is above feet.

4a. Choke up (grip lower) on club.

b. Check ball position.

5. You top sidehill shots with ball below feet.

5a. Check setup position; you may be sitting back too much on heels.

b. Put weight on heels but maintain posture over ball (see Figure 9.2).

6. You consistently pull sidehill lies when ball is above feet.

6a. Check alignment.

b. Ball tends to curve in direction down slope (hook).

Uneven Lie Drills

1. Setup Sidehill Lie Drill

To become familiar with the setup position for sidehill lies, find a sidehill lie from which to practice. Place two clubs on the grass, one lying straight up the slope, the other at right angles to this (see Figures 9.2a and b). These clubs provide a reference for ball position and stance. Choose a target to the right or left of the horizontal club.

Using a 5-iron, modify your setup for the slope of the hill. Practice swings, noting the way your swing feels and the sensations of the swing. Do you feel balanced?

Success Goal = 20 total swings while noting balance on the follow-through

10 swings from sidehill lies, balls below feet

10 swings from sidehill lies, balls above feet

Your Score =
(#) _____ swings from sidehill lies, ball below feet

(#) _____ of these swings in balance

(#) _____ swings from sidehill lies, ball above feet

(#) _____ of these swings in balance

2. Uphill/Downhill Lie Drill

To become familiar with uphill and downhill lies, find such lies from which to practice. Place two clubs on the grass, one lying straight up the slope, the other at right angles to this (see Figures 9.3a and b). These clubs provide a reference for ball position and stance. Choose targets to the high side of the club lying up the slope for the uphill lie and to the low side of this club for the downhill lie.

Using a 5-iron, modify your setup for the slope of the hill. Note your sensations on the swing. Do you feel balanced in the follow-through?

Success Goal = 20 total swings, while noting balance on the follow-through

10 swings, downhill lie

10 swings, uphill lie

Your Score =
(#) _____ swings, downhill lie

(#) _____ of these swings in balance

(#) _____ swings, uphill lie

(#) _____ of these swings in balance

3. Single Bucket Drill

In order to gain an awareness of the desired ascending and descending angles of approach, on flat ground place one foot on a bucket or the edge of your golf bag. Note how each swing feels as the bucket or golf bag limits your lower body action and exaggerates the sense of ascent or descent of the swing.

a. To feel the descending angle of approach with the irons, take your regular setup position for the full swing with a ball in the center of your stance and on a tee. Place your rear foot on the bucket. Hit balls using a 7-iron, noting how it feels.

b. To feel the ascending angle, take your regular setup position with the ball on a tee toward your target side. Place your target-side foot on the bucket. Hit balls with a 5- or 7-wood.

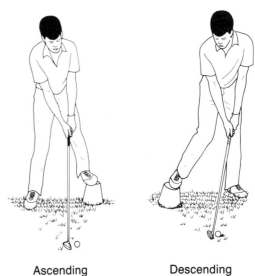

Ascending   Descending

Success Goal = 10 total swings

5 swings with a 7-iron, your rear foot on bucket

5 swings with a 5- or 7-iron, ball on tee, target-side foot on bucket

Your Score =

(#) _____ balls hit with 7-iron

(#) _____ balls hit with 5- or 7-wood

4. Cluster Drill

Distance and accuracy control in short shots can be affected by uneven lies. The back areas of practice greens and tees can provide good practice areas for these shots.

a. Using a pitching wedge or 9-iron, practice the pitch shot from each type of uneven lie. Try to emphasize consistency in distance and direction, trying to group the balls within 5 yards of each other from about 25 yards away. Be sure to use your full setup routine before each shot.

b. Using a 9- or 7-iron, practice the chip shot from each of the uneven lies. Hit balls for consistency in distance and direction. Be sure to use your full setup routine before each shot.

Success Goal = 40 total shots from uneven lies

a. 20 total pitch shots, grouping balls into 5-yard cluster

    5 pitches from uphill lie

    5 pitches from downhill lie

    5 pitches from sidehill lie, balls below feet

    5 pitches from sidehill lie, balls above feet

b. 20 total chip shots, grouping balls into 5-yard cluster

    5 chips from uphill lie

    5 chips from downhill lie

    5 chips from sidehill lie, balls below feet

    5 chips from sidehill lie, balls above feet

Your Score =

a. (#) _____ pitches from uphill lie

   (#) _____ pitches from downhill lie

   (#) _____ pitches from sidehill lie, balls below feet

   (#) _____ pitches from sidehill lie, balls above feet

b. (#) _____ chips from uphill lie

   (#) _____ chips from downhill lie

   (#) _____ chips from sidehill lie, balls below feet

   (#) _____ chips from sidehill lie, balls above feet

Uneven Lies
Keys to Success Checklists

You have been testing yourself by attaining each of the uneven lie Success Goals. Next ask your teacher, your coach, or another trained observer to qualitatively evaluate your technique according to the two checklists below— one is for sidehill lies, the other for up- or downhill lies. Asterisks (*) on the sidehill lie checklist note the differences in the setup positions of the balls above and below the feet compared with the regular full swing setup discussed in Step 3. Ask the observer to check off each item as it appears.

Sidehill Lies
(ball either above or below feet)

Preparation Phase

Setup

Ball above feet

Ball below feet

Ball Above Feet	Ball Below Feet	
	_____	Grip neutral
* _____		Grip regular, choked-up
_____	_____	Feet shoulder width apart
_____	_____	Weight evenly distributed
* _____		Weight even
	* _____	Weight toward heels
* _____	* _____	Alignment square to intermediate target line:
_____	_____	Feet
_____	_____	Hips
_____	_____	Shoulders
_____	_____	Posture with flat back
_____	_____	Eyes over hand Ball position:
_____	_____	Irons: center of stance
_____	_____	Woods: target side of center
* _____	* _____	Blade of club square to intermediate target line

Execution
Phase

Ball Above Feet	*Ball Below Feet*	**Backswing**
____	____	Arms, hands, club swing back as unit
____	____	Weight shifts to rear (target knee touches rear knee)
____	____	Wrists cocked at hip level
____	____	Hips turn to rear (belt buckle back)
____	____	Backswing length 4 or 5
____	____	Heel of target foot off ground slightly
____	____	Hands over rear shoulder at full turn
____	____	Club parallel to ground (5)

Ball Above Feet	*Ball Below Feet*	**Forwardswing**
____	____	Weight shift to target side:
____	____	Target heel down
____	____	Target knee toward target
____	____	Hips return to square
____	____	Arms, hands, club swing down as unit
____	____	Wrists uncock at hip level
____	____	Rear knee turned, touching target knee
____	____	Wrists recock at target-side hip level
____	____	Hips turned to target (belt buckle turned toward target)

Follow-Through
Phase

Ball Above Feet	*Ball Below Feet*	
____	____	Swing continues smoothly
____	____	Arms, hands, club continue until hands higher than target shoulder
____	____	Hips face target
____	____	Forwardswing length 4 or 5
____	____	Chest to target
____	____	Holds position at end to check for balance

Uphill or Downhill Lies (ball even with feet)

Preparation Phase

Setup

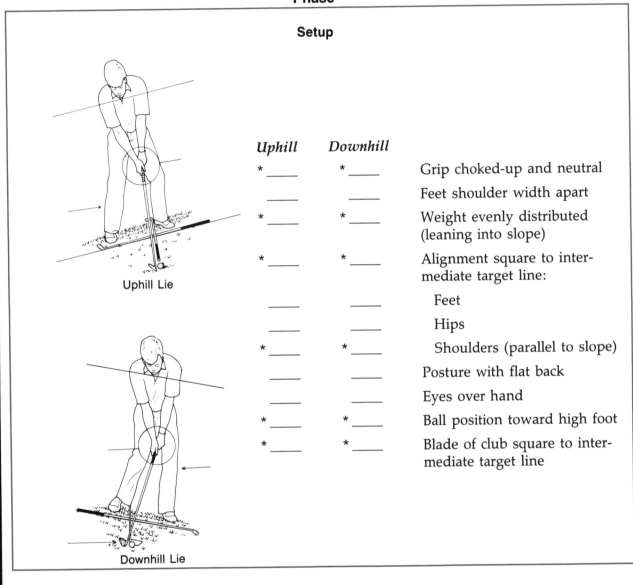

Uphill Lie

Downhill Lie

Uphill	Downhill	
*_____	*_____	Grip choked-up and neutral
_____	_____	Feet shoulder width apart
*_____	*_____	Weight evenly distributed (leaning into slope)
*_____	*_____	Alignment square to intermediate target line:
_____	_____	Feet
_____	_____	Hips
*_____	*_____	Shoulders (parallel to slope)
_____	_____	Posture with flat back
_____	_____	Eyes over hand
*_____	*_____	Ball position toward high foot
*_____	*_____	Blade of club square to intermediate target line

Execution
Phase

Backswing

Uphill	*Downhill*	
——	——	Arms, hands, club swing back as unit
——	——	Weight shifts to rear (target knee touches rear knee)
——	——	Wrists cocked at hip level
——	——	Hips turn to rear (belt buckle back)
——	——	Backswing length 4 or 5
——	——	Heel of target foot off ground slightly
——	——	Hands over rear shoulder at full turn
——	——	Club parallel to ground (5)

Forwardswing

Uphill	*Downhill*	
——	——	Weight shift to target side:
——	——	Target heel down
——	——	Target knee toward target
——	——	Hips return to square
——	——	Arms, hands, club swing down as unit
——	——	Wrists uncock at hip level
——	——	Rear knee turned, touching target knee
——	——	Wrists recock at target-side hip level
——	——	Hips turned to target (belt buckle turned toward target)

Follow-Through
Phase

Uphill	Downhill	
____	____	Swing continues smoothly
____	____	Arms, hands, club continue until hands higher than target shoulder
____	____	Hips face target
____	____	Forwardswing length 4 or 5
____	____	Chest to target
____	____	Holds position at end to check for balance

Step 10 **Effective Practice**

Effective practice in golf requires that you systematically work to make the fundamental skills automatic and then learn to apply them in many different situations. An integrated approach to golf means that you must take what you have learned in the preceding steps of this book, practice those skills individually, and then create sequences that are similar to those you experience on the golf course.

WHY IS EFFECTIVE PRACTICE IMPORTANT?

Golf is different from many other sports due to the individual shots that you execute at your own pace. You are not required to respond to the pace of a moving object or to react to another player's motions. However, you must be able to respond to the various environmental situations that occur in golf, such as various ball lies, distances to targets, and irregular terrains. Therefore, during practice you should practice isolated techniques as well as the variations that can occur on the golf course. It is possible to practice almost every conceivable shot in practice, so why not take advantage of this opportunity?

HOW TO PRACTICE EFFECTIVELY

The first few minutes of practice should always be spent *preparing your body for success*. Before each practice, be sure to use the two-phase warm-up routine discussed in the first section of this book. Work all of your body parts, focusing on flexibility. This helps you feel the stretch of your muscles and be ready to "tune in" to your body during practice.

Start every practice session under the best conditions possible. Find a nice grassy area and practice with your best shots. This allows you to develop a smooth and repeatable swing, which can then be adapted to special course circumstances. Start your practice with the mid-irons first, then short irons, and finally long irons and woods. Be sure to have clear target lines so that your alignment is the same for all shots. With each practice stroke, determine your target, focus on your posture and smooth swing, and watch the ball flight.

Start by placing a club on the ground pointing toward a target. Remember, golf is a target game, and you must have a target each time in order to learn from the flight of your golf ball. Put your ball on a tee about 1/2 inch above the ground when practicing the full swing. This assures a consistent ball lie as you develop your swing techniques. When you have achieved 50% consistency in ball flight during practice with your ball on a tee, alternate 3 swings with the tee and 2 swings with the ball on the ground. As you hit the ball, watch the ball flight. Was it straight? Did it curve? Did it travel as far as you thought it should? Use the feedback from each ball flight to check your basic skills (see Step 4 for a review). Effective practice keys are presented in Figure 10.1.

Figure 10.1   Keys to Success: *Effective Practice*

**Preparation
Phase**

a

1. Warm up
2. Use alignment club
3. Ball on tee

**Full Swing
Techniques**

1. Mid-irons first (5–7)
2. Short irons (8–9)

3. Long irons (3–4)
4. Wedges (pitching and sand)

**Target
Awareness**

b

1. Identify specific target
2. Use alignment club
3. Learn from ball flight cues
4. Use preswing routine

**Setup
Position**

c

1. Grip
2. Stance

   Check body alignment:
   a. Feet
   b. Hips
   c. Shoulders
3. Clubface alignment

If you notice that various shots travel straight but off-target, you may have an alignment problem or may be swinging the club in an unusual path. If the ball curves in flight, it may be due to the position of the clubface at impact, which varies because of the actions of the arms and hands. If the ball seems to fly too high or never gets off the ground, it may be due to the angle of approach (the downward swing of the club) or the point on the ball that the clubhead hits (below or above the center of the ball). These cues were discussed in Step 4 and can be reviewed during your practice.

There are also many specific drills that are great for practice. Review the drills presented in Steps 1 through 9. These are excellent practice exercises that allow you to feel comfortable with your swing and make it an "automatic" skill. Remember, the keys to developing a good golf swing are to be able to do the same thing each time and to sense what you did differently if the ball did not travel the way you intended.

When you decide to practice on your own, choose one or two aspects of your shot to work on. For example, if you are having difficulty getting enough distance from your shots, you may want to check to be sure that you have good body rotation and weight shift to allow a free swing. Exercises from previous steps such as the Wide-Whoosher Drill (Step 3) and the Body Rotation Drill (Step 1) would be very helpful. On the other hand, if you seem to lose your balance, try the One-Leg Toe Drill (Step 3) to learn to keep your swing centered, which aids your balance.

When you use a drill, it is important to combine it with actual strokes. For example, practice the Cocking Drill Without a Ball (Step 3) 5 times. Then take 5 actual strokes. Then repeat the drill again, followed by 5 more actual strokes. Then repeat the drill twice, and hit 5 times, and finally just hit 10 balls in a row to finish the practice.

It is important that you finish each practice session wanting to come back for another one. Some teachers suggest that for the last few shots of the day, you should focus on executing the most perfect swing possible. Once you have executed one of your best shots, stop. This allows you to walk away feeling good, remembering that great shot. Don't worry about hitting every single ball in your pile—it is better to have a great memory to store away, to savor the good feel of a good shot. Remember, replace the bad shots (by hitting or imagining good ones), and remember the good shots for future reference.

Realistic Practice Drills

Once you have warmed up and practiced your perfect technique, practice this technique in a more gamelike situation. Early in practice, you should repeat the same shot over and over again, generally striving for at least 50% success. After you have warmed up though, you should practice a variety of shots. Remember, in golf you never hit a ball from the same place twice.

Because golf is a target game, it is important to practice aiming toward a variety of targets. As part of your practice routine, you should consider varying two elements: the target and the club selection.

1. Routine Practice

It is very important that every shot in golf start from the same basic setup sequence. For this reason, it is critical to practice your setup routine with each shot. In this drill, focus on the use of your routine, and the feel of the swing. Keep track of the number of times you are able to repeat exactly the same routine.

Success Goal = hitting 20 balls, using same setup routine each time

Your Score = number of times in 20 shots that you used each element of the standard routine

Assessing shot demands

    1. (#) _____ determine lie of ball

    2 (#) _____ determine desired trajectory

    3. (#) _____ determine distance to target

    4. (#) _____ select club to match the demands of the lie, trajectory, and distance (LTD)

Standing behind ball

    5. (#) _____ establish grip

    6. (#) _____ select target landing area

    7. (#) _____ select intermediate target

Standing to side of ball

    8. (#) _____ relocate intermediate target

    9. (#) _____ align club with intermediate target

    10. (#) _____ set feet

    11. (#) _____ get comfortable

    12. (#) _____ clear mind

2. *Varying the Target Drill*

Start this drill by working with one club at a time (irons first, then woods). Select an iron of your choice. For example, take a 5-iron and use it to practice the full swing motion at one target, then vary the target location. Aim at a target that is to the left or right of your practice location, as well as one that is straight ahead.

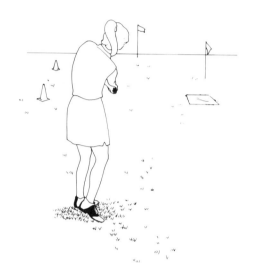

Success Goal = 20 total swings toward targets with a full swing motion

5 swings straight ahead

5 swings to target to left

5 swings to target to right

1 swing straight ahead

1 swing to left

1 swing to right

1 swing to left

1 swing straight ahead

Your Score =

(#) _____ swings straight ahead (5)

(#) _____ swings to target to left (5)

(#) _____ swings to target to right (5)

(#) _____ swing straight ahead (1)

(#) _____ swing to target to left (1)

(#) _____ swing to target to right (1)

(#) _____ swing to target to left (1)

(#) _____ swing straight ahead (1)

3. Varying the Club Drill

Using various clubs, practice aiming at close targets, targets far away, and intermediate targets. Feel the difference in swing sensations due to the lengths of the clubs selected for a particular distance. (Review the distance drills in each step.)

Success Goal = hitting toward three different targets, using a good full swing each time

  5 swings with 5-iron at target 120 yards away

  5 swings with 7-iron at target 100 yards away

  5 swings with 3-iron at target 150 yards away

  2 swings with 5-iron at 120 yards

  2 swings with 7-iron at 100 yards

  2 swings with 3-iron at 150 yards

  1 swing with 5-iron at 120 yards

  1 swing with 7-iron at 100 yards

  1 swing with 3-iron at 150 yards

Your Score =

  (#) _____ swings with 5-iron at 120 yards (5)

  (#) _____ swings with 7-iron at 100 yards (5)

  (#) _____ swings with 3-iron at 150 yards (5)

  (#) _____ swings with 5-iron at 120 yards (2)

  (#) _____ swings with 7-iron at 100 yards (2)

  (#) _____ swings with 3-iron at 150 yards (2)

  (#) _____ swing with 5-iron at 120 yards (1)

  (#) _____ swing with 7-iron at 100 yards (1)

  (#) _____ swing with 3-iron at 150 yards (1)

4. Vary the Lie of the Ball Drill

Practice areas do not always have the variety of ball lies found on a course, such as uneven lies or high grass as in roughs. These need to be practiced whenever possible, even if only with practice swings.

Most practice areas have good lies when the ball sits on top of the grass and bad lies when the ball rests on bare ground or in divot holes. When you hit a shot from these lies, notice the differences in how it feels when you strike the ball and how the ball flies after it is struck.

Success Goal = 25 total swings from good and bad lies

   5 swings from good lie

   5 swings from bare spot

   5 swings from good lie

   5 swings from divot hole

   5 swings from good lie

Your Score =

   (#) _____ swings from good lie

   (#) _____ swings from bare spot

   (#) _____ swings from good lie

   (#) _____ swings from divot hole

   (#) _____ swings from good lie

5. Opposites Drill

It is important to be able to match the way extreme shots feel with what causes them to happen. In order to do that, identify pairs of opposite types of ball flight results: slices and hooks, topping the ball and hitting it "fat," and pushes and pulls.

Alternate hitting shots within each pair of opposites. For example, hit one slice and then one hook, or push one and then pull one shot. After hitting 3 sets of one pair of opposites, hit 6 good shots. Then go on to the next pair. Make each shot as different from its opposite as possible, for example, a big hook and a big slice.

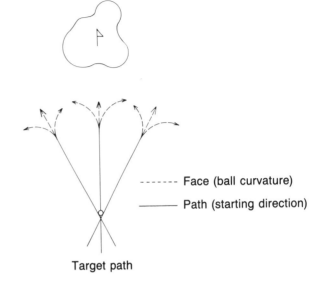

------- Face (ball curvature)

———— Path (starting direction)

Target path

Success Goal = 36 total shots, hitting each pair 3 times (6 swings), with at least 4 of 6 attempts correct on each pair

　6 shots alternating slice and hook

　6 good shots

　6 shots alternating hitting on top of the ball and hitting fat

　6 good shots

　6 shots alternating push and pull

　6 good shots

Your Score =

　(#) _____ slice versus hook

　(#) _____ good shots

　(#) _____ topping versus hitting fat

　(#) _____ good shots

　(#) _____ pushing versus pulling

　(#) _____ good shots

6. Pitch and Chip Drill

Feeling comfortable with the short game in golf is critical to success. Practice acquiring a comfortable feel with both pitching and chipping by executing each shot 10 times, then alternating them to sense the different feelings.

Pitching

Chipping

Success Goal = 30 total shots using pitching or chipping

    10 shots with a pitching wedge or 9-iron at a pitching target 30–50 yards away

    10 shots chipping with a 5- or 7-iron at a chipping target 10 yards away

    3 shots pitching

    3 shots chipping

    2 shots pitching

    2 shots chipping

Your Score =

    (#) _____ pitched with PW or 9 iron (10)

    (#) _____ chipped with 5 or 7 iron (10)

    (#) _____ pitched (3)

    (#) _____ chipped (3)

    (#) _____ pitched (2)

    (#) _____ chipped (2)

7. Round of Golf Drill

Imagine each shot of a golf hole, picking out a target in your practice field for each one. Using your complete setup routine with each shot, hit the same sequence of real shots you would hit on the actual course. Never use the same two clubs in a row (unless you whiff one). Shift the target each time. This is the most realistic form of practice and should be done during each practice session.

Imagine that you are playing a round of golf from the practice tee. Look out into the practice field and imagine an entire hole. The round starts on the first hole, perhaps a par 4. Start with a wood, or perhaps an iron if you are more comfortable with it. Actually hit the ball with that club. Follow this by perhaps a 5-iron on your second shot or, if you hit the first shot a long way, a 7- or 8-iron. Continue playing real shots until you have reached the green of the imaginary hole. Then take out a putter and stroke the ball toward the target you had chosen while on the practice tee. In your mind, see the ball go into the hole. Go on to the next tee.

Record the clubs used for each shot and the resultant ball flight. Also place an ''R'' near the club number if you used your routine.

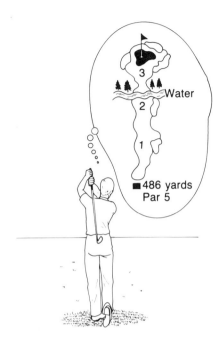

Strategy for playing Par 5

1. Tee off with 5-wood
2. 7-wood short of water
3. 5-iron to green with safe area between

Success Goal = playing 9 holes, selecting (and recording) a different shot and club each time, drawing shot diagrams for each ''hole,'' and completing your entire routine with each swing

Your Score = clubs used and routine utilization on each of the 9 holes you imagined and played in a realistic fashion.

Hole 1: _____ clubs used, _____ routine done

Hole 2: _____ clubs used, _____ routine done

Hole 3: _____ clubs used, _____ routine done

Hole 4: _____ clubs used, _____ routine done

Hole 5: _____ clubs used, _____ routine done

Hole 6: _____ clubs used, _____ routine done

Hole 7: _____ clubs used, _____ routine done

Hole 8: _____ clubs used, _____ routine done

Hole 9: _____ clubs used, _____ routine done

Step 11 **Preshot Routines for Each Swing**

Each golf swing is a separate, self-paced movement. Because you have complete control over the preparation for each shot, this aspect can be almost identical for each shot and can therefore serve as a reliable, and repeatable, first step. Your preparation routine should be practiced so much that it becomes an automatic aspect of each shot, that you go through it even though distracted or under pressure of competition.

WHY IS A PRESHOT ROUTINE IMPORTANT?

When you watch a tennis player serve or a basketball player shoot a free throw, have you ever noticed that they bounce the ball the same number of times before each attempt? This is not a superstitious behavior; it is part of their preshot preparation and serves as a signal to the body that it is time for action. If you do the same thing before each shot, you can check that you are ready for the swing and also be sure that your body is in a position to act.

In golf, a preshot routine should include selecting a target and club, concentrating, and taking the setup. You may do some things that make you feel especially relaxed and comfortable, and they may be different from what

someone else does. The key to success is that *you do the same things before each shot.*

HOW TO ESTABLISH A PRESHOT ROUTINE

Each golfer's preshot routine is unique to that individual. Though there are some aspects that are included in every good routine, the order of the aspects and some specific characteristics differ from golfer to golfer. For one golfer, though, the aspects of the routine should always take place in the same order and take about the same amount of time for every shot.

Most preshot routines in golf consist of three parts: selection of target and club, self-monitoring (relaxation, tension control, concentration, and imagery), and setup.

Because golf is a target game, one of the most important aspects of your preshot routine is to decide on the target and select the club. You can do this most easily by focusing on three things: selecting the target while you stand behind the ball, selecting a club to match the demands of the desired shot, and choosing an intermediate target for alignment (see Figure 11.1).

Figure 11.1   Keys to Success:
Preshot Routine

**Target
Selection**

a

1. Stand behind ball
2. Select target or landing area
3. Select intermediate target 12–18 inches ahead of ball on target line

**Club
Selection**

b

1. Determine distance to target
2. Determine trajectory
3. Determine the lie of ball
4. Select club to match distance and flight

**Alignment With
Intermediate Target**

c

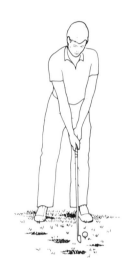

1. Relocate intermediate target from side of ball
2. Align club with intermediate target 12–18 inches on the target side of the ball
3. Align body to club
4. Set feet

The second aspect of a good routine involves being able to control your attention and relax before each shot. Self-monitoring means being able to relax your body to its prime level and focus on the swing itself. There are three aspects of self-control that are particularly important: tension control, concentration, and imagery.

The importance of understanding self-control in golf cannot be overstated. Because golf is a completely self-paced activity, it is easy for outside tensions or distractions to influence performance. You must therefore learn to let your body "run off" the swings, and without interference from distracting thoughts or influences. While playing golf it is easy to be distracted and to let your mind wander. Thoughts and feelings that are not related to the shot you are about to make can easily interfere with your performance. It is therefore important to learn to control your attention and to focus on the decisions you must make

regarding the landing area, club selection, and smooth swing.

WHY IS CONCENTRATION IMPORTANT?

Distracting thoughts may be related to many different things, including loud noises, thoughts about previous shots missed, daydreams about future shots, being angry at yourself for a dumb mistake, or concern over what someone else might be thinking about you. None of those types of thoughts can help with the shot you are about to hit. Instead, you should think only about the shot at hand.

If you find that you are not concentrating on this shot or are thinking nonproductive thoughts, STOP. Use a technique called *thought stoppage*. Its first aspect is to recognize negative thoughts. Immediately stop them and simply replace them with self-enhancing thoughts (see Figure 11.2).

Figure 11.2   Keys to Success:
Concentration

**Recognize
Negative Thoughts**

a

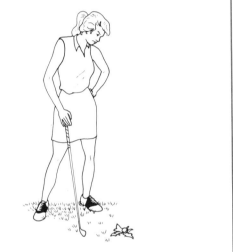

1. Identify negative
   thoughts
2. Identify lack of concentration

**Use Trigger
to Stop Negative Thoughts**

b

1. Use trigger to abruptly
   stop negative thought
   (snap fingers, slap, etc.)
2. Take deep breath
3. Exhale to regain control
   and blow out self-doubts

**Replace Bad Thoughts
With Good Thoughts**

c

1. Make positive statement
2. Refocus on present

SETUP

The setup was described in Step 2 in order that you might prepare your body to execute a good swing. The points that were critical in that setup should now be automatic and can be integrated into a standard routine. Each time you take your setup, it should be done in the same sequence. It can be thought of in terms of three parts: aim, posture, mental control (see Figure 11.3). Once you have done this routine, just "let it happen." Remember, the ball is only getting in the way of your natural swing, so do not try to steer it or actively hit it.

Each routine should include the taking of a practice swing. If you use one, be sure to take it from the side of the ball in the same alignment you would use to actually hit the ball. Stand about 1 foot away from the ball and make a practice swing at the normal pace (not in slow motion). Then take one step forward, align the clubface to the intermediate target, get comfortable, reset your feet, and continue with your routine.

Figure 11.3   Keys to Success:
Setup

Aim

a

1. Select target from behind ball
2. Select intermediate target from behind
3. Grip club
4. Practice swing

Posture

b

1. Align clubface*
2. Set feet, target-side foot first
3. Get comfortable
4. Check target

* Remember not to ground club in hazard

Mental Control

c

1. Clear mind, relax
2. Use a swing cue word

3. Swing
4. Hold follow-through

Detecting Routine Errors

The use of a standard routine before each shot is a skill just like any of the other skills you have practiced. When you skip part of the routine or allow it to be disrupted, you must stop and start the full routine over again. It is therefore important to be able to detect problems in your routine.

ERROR   **CORRECTION**

1. You change target line by realigning feet after addressing ball, (i.e., you have second thoughts about the target selection).

1. STOP. Go back behind ball and check that the proper intermediate target was selected. Repeat remaining aspects of routine without second thoughts or doubts.

2. You adjust grip at setup after aligning club.

2. STOP. Go back behind ball and take grip by holding arms horizontally as in regular routine.

ERROR

CORRECTION

3. You look around or speak to someone during routine.

3. STOP. Step back from ball, take practice swing; then realign clubface with intermediate target and continue routine.

4. Walking up to ball and seeing water hazard about 100 yards ahead, you visualize next shot landing in water.

4. STOP. Use thought stoppage, replacing negative thought with self-enhancing thought; then proceed with routine.

Routine Drills

1. Intermediate Target Drill

Pick a target in your practice field. Stand behind the ball and select an intermediate target about 8–12 inches ahead of the ball. Place a piece of tape between the ball and target and return to the rear of ball to check the line of the target.

Success Goal = 10 alignments with intermediate target in line with target

Your Score = (#) _____ alignments

2. Partner Distraction Drill

Working with a partner, take turns taking shots while the other says distracting things or tosses paper, tees, or grass into the shooter's visual field. Being able to adjust to and ignore such distractions is good concentration practice. Using a 5-iron, hit 10 balls toward a selected target, using your routine each time.

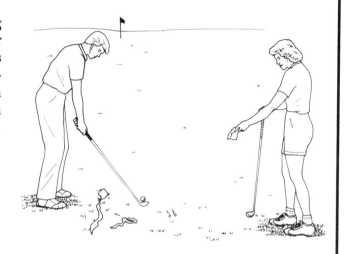

Success Goal = hitting 10 balls with entire routine, maintaining concentration in spite of partner's attempts to distract

Your Score = (#) _____ balls hit while maintaining concentration

3. Circle Alignment Drill

In order to appreciate the value of your routine, try hitting 10 balls without using your routine. Walk up to the ball, walk around it twice, take your setup, aim at a target, and swing. Noticing where the ball lands, set your club on the ground along your toes and walk back to check how close your alignment was to the desired target line. Notice whether you tend to aim to the right or left of the desired target; this is your *bias*.

Success Goal = 20 total alignments

   10 without a routine, noting your alignment bias each time

   10 using your alignment routine each time

Your Score =

   a. Without using a routine, note whether each shot is on target or with alignment bias to right or to left

Shot	Alignment bias or result
1.	_____
2.	_____
3.	_____
4.	_____
5.	_____
6.	_____
7.	_____
8.	_____
9.	_____
10.	_____

b. Using routine each time, check whether on target or with a bias
1. _____ on target; or biased to _____
2. _____ on target; or biased to _____
3. _____ on target; or biased to _____
4. _____ on target; or biased to _____
5. _____ on target; or biased to _____
6. _____ on target; or biased to _____
7. _____ on target; or biased to _____
8. _____ on target; or biased to _____
9. _____ on target; or biased to _____
10. _____ on target; or biased to _____

4. Routine Timing Drill

With a partner, take turns timing your entire routine. At first, be sure to repeat it the same way each time. Then try speeding up the routine so that it is twice as fast. Notice what happens to your concentration, swing pace, and accuracy. Time the routine 10 times: 4 times at normal speed, 3 times fast, and 3 times back at normal speed. During the last 3 trials, try to come within 10% of the average times for shots 1-4.

Success Goal = repeating the same routine 10 times, noting the differences in feel and results, and finally, staying within 10% of your normal time during the last three attempts

4 times at regular speed

3 times faster than normal

3 times back at regular speed

Your Score =

Routine at regular speed	Time
1	_____
2	_____
3	_____
4	_____
Total	_____
Average	Determine Average plus 10% = _____ ; Average minus 10% = _____

Routine at fast speed	Time	How do these feel different?
5	_____	_____
6	_____	_____
7	_____	_____

Routine at regular speed	Time	Check if speed good (within 10% of average)	Check if too fast	Check if too slow
8	_____	_____	_____	_____
9	_____	_____	_____	_____
10	_____	_____	_____	_____

Preshot Routine Keys to Success Checklist

Having a consistent and repeatable preshot routine allows you to start each swing in the same way. It makes it much easier for you to be relaxed and ready to hit the shot, and able to learn from the flight of your golf ball. The preshot routine should include aspects of club selection, target selection, and alignment.

Ask a partner or friend to check to see whether you follow the same routine each time.

Club Selection

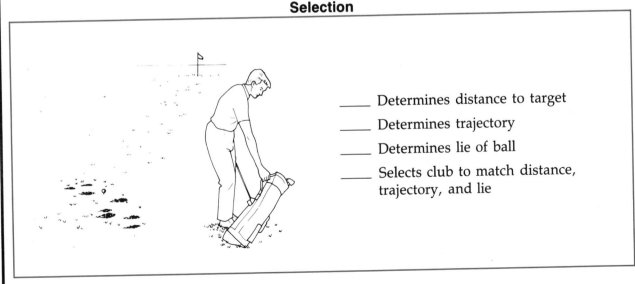

_____ Determines distance to target

_____ Determines trajectory

_____ Determines lie of ball

_____ Selects club to match distance, trajectory, and lie

Target Selection

_____ Stands behind ball

_____ Establishes grip on club

_____ Selects target or landing area

_____ Selects intermediate target 12–18 inches ahead of ball on target line

Aligns Body With Intermediate Target

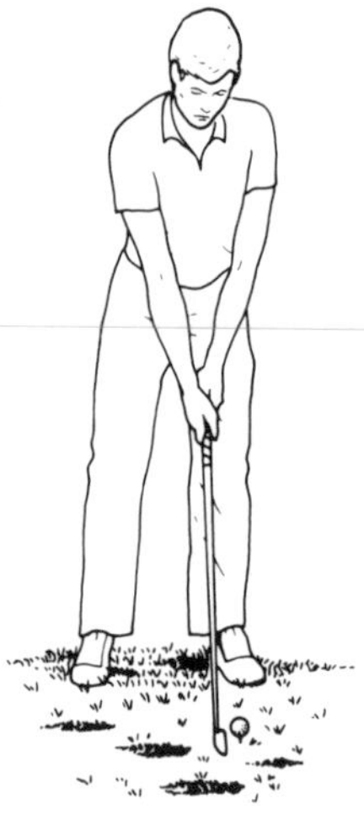

_____ Practices swing at side of ball

_____ Relocates intermediate target from side of ball

_____ Aligns club with intermediate target

_____ Aligns body to club

_____ Sets feet (rear-foot first)

_____ Gets comfortable

Clears Mind

_____ Clears mind

_____ Uses swing cue or visual image of shot

Step 12   Preparing for a Round of Golf: Mental Skills

All golfers must learn how to prepare for a round of golf. The game of golf requires not only the physical skills you have practiced in the previous sections, but also mental skills to direct your body into executing the physical skills. Because golf requires both strength and precision, it is important that you learn to relax as you prepare to hit your golf shots. This step provides you with a method to optimize your level of body tension and prepare for a round of golf.

If your strokes have problematic results, the cause may be your swing or things in your mind that cause tension and get in the way of the swing. It is therefore important to practice both the mental and physical aspects of your swing.

WHY IS TENSION CONTROL IMPORTANT?

One of your biggest golf problems may be you are trying too hard. When you really want to hit that shot well, or when there is a small safe-landing area and all you can see is the water hazard or the traps surrounding the green, you must be able to control your reactions. If you are distracted by such challenges, you may make poor shots because of the tension, which can affect your hands and shoulders.

Watch the flight of a golf ball when you are really nervous or tense. Imagine where the ball would go if you held onto the club like a hammer—a ''white knuckle grip.'' If you grip your club too tightly, you cannot release your hands through the area of impact with the ball; the result is a slice. How do we know that? Remember when you observed the ball flights in Step 4—we discussed the fact that when a ball curves as it flies through the air, it is because of spin imparted due to clubface position. The most common error is a slice, which occurs when the hands do not release and the face of the club is therefore open.

Sometimes you do not realize that there is excess tension, because we do not have specific words to describe a variety of tension levels. You can see the result of tension when you hit a slice, though, because your grip is so tight—a gorilla grip—it makes your knuckles white. Some golfers also perceive tension by the end of a practice session or round of golf, when their hands feel achey.

It is important to learn to feel this tension problem, so you can control it before it controls the flight of your golf ball. In order to understand what happens when you are tense and to be able to feel when tension is a problem, practice this exercise: Imagine that the best, semirelaxed grip on a golf club is a 3, a much too tight grip is a 5, and a very loose grip is a 1. Now hit a few golf balls using 5, 3, and 1 grips. (Just be careful that with a 1, you do not let the club fly out of your hands!) Compare the different feels and results.

HOW TO CONTROL TENSION

The keys to tension control (see Figure 12.1) are being able to keep your body in a balanced range of dynamic tension (3) and detecting when it gets outside of that optimal range. If one part of your body is too tense, for example, your hands or shoulders, you can learn to correct the tension level in much the same way that you corrected your slice or hook. A technique called *progressive relaxation* takes advantage of the same principle of ''playing in the extremes to find the means'' that you practiced before. Start by tensing your muscles to the maximum (5), then relax them completely (1). Then find the medium level of tension at 3.

When you find yourself with excess tension, take a deep breath and exhale fully. This physiological mechanism signals your body that you are in control. Try it. Make a very tight fist with both hands (5) and then take a big, deep breath. Now exhale fully and release the tension in your hands. This deep breathing technique is a very powerful signal to your body and can become a good method for you to use. Whenever you feel tense, take a deep breath, exhale, and then regain control to the medium level of 3.

Figure 12.1 Keys to Success: Tension Control

Detecting Tension

a

1. Neck and shoulders
2. Hands (grip)
3. Back
4. Legs

a   Maximum Tension (5)   b   Medium Tension (3)

Selective Relaxation

b
1. Take a deep breath
2. Exhale fully and smile
3. Tension level 3 in neck and shoulders

4. Tension level 3 in hands (grip)
5. Tension level 3 in back
6. Tension level 3 in legs

Detecting Tension Errors

The flight of your golf ball can tell a great deal about both your physical performance and your mental approach to golf. As was discussed in Step 4, the flight of your ball can be used to detect many problems with your golf swing. The flights of your golf balls are affected not only directly by your physical swing but also indirectly by mental processes influencing physical technique. If mental tension causes you to grip your club too tightly, you cannot release your hand through the area of impact with the ball; a slice results. Similarly, if you constantly top the ball, it may be because of too much tension in your shoulders, which could be alleviated by conscious relaxation. The errors listed below represent the most common problems related to tension control.

ERROR

CORRECTION

1. You have too much tension on backswing, causing you to top ball.

1. Keep arms at medium tension (level 3).

ERROR   **CORRECTION**

2. Grip is too loose at top, causing collapse at ball or hitting ground behind ball.

2. Keep grip at desired level of tension (3) throughout swing.

3. You have too much tension in shoulders, causing you to top ball.

3. Keep shoulders at optimal level (3).

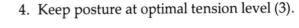

ERROR   **CORRECTION**

4. Lower body and legs give in (flex), causing club to hit ground behind ball.

4. Keep posture at optimal tension level (3).

WHY IS ATTENTIONAL CONTROL IMPORTANT?

Perhaps the greatest challenge in playing the game of golf is keeping your attention focused on what you are doing. When you are playing golf, you may be distracted because of the hazards ahead, the weather, your perceived strengths and weaknesses, or other things on your mind. You may start to worry that someone else is watching you, that a friend may make fun of you, or that you may embarrass yourself. None of these worries can help your golf swing; in fact, they can only get in your way.

Instead of worrying or doubting your own decisions, you must have faith in what you know and trust in the swing you have developed. This means practicing as well as you can and then letting that practice expertise come out when you play. It never helps to worry about what might have been if only you had practiced harder, or about whether you hit an earlier shot better. Nor does it help to daydream about what might come true. In-stead, focus on what you are doing, decide what shot to hit, and then relax and let your skills run off automatically.

HOW TO EXECUTE ATTENTIONAL CONTROL

Maintaining attentional control is a skill as important as any physical skill you demonstrate in your golf game. It must be practiced by using a preshot routine and being sure that your thoughts remain in the present tense, rather than worrying about the past or dreaming about the future. It is not possible to maintain absolute attention throughout an entire round of golf (sometimes as long as 4–6 hours), but it is critical to establish attentional control as part of your preshot routine at least. It would therefore help to establish a cue that triggers your routine, such as coming up to your ball, setting down your golf bag, or parking your cart (see Figure 12.2).

Figure 12.2   Keys to Success: *Maintaining Attention*

Attentional Cue

a

1. Set down bag as signal
2. Clear mind
3. Select cue

Preshot Routine

b

1. Select target
2. Select club
3. Grip club while standing behind ball
4. Choose intermediate target
5. Take practice swing
6. Align clubface
7. Set feet and get comfortable
8. Check target

Execution

c

1. Clear thoughts (use
   swing cue)
2. Swing
3. Hold follow-through

Detecting Attentional Errors

Listening to your own self-talk is the key to detecting attentional errors. If you hear yourself questioning your skills, discussing what is to come later, or how you played the last few holes, you are not in control of your attention.

ERROR   **CORRECTION**

1. When standing on tee overlooking water hazard, thoughts focus on possible lost ball; when driven, sure enough—ball goes into water.

1. Think about and see safe landing areas, not possible problem; imagine ball landing safely.

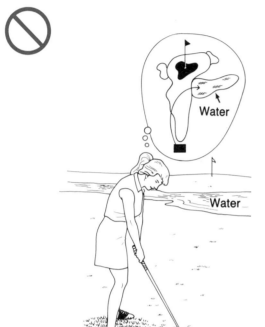

2. You think about great round you are playing, then whiff ball.

2. Focus on present shot; use entire routine and swing cue "smooth."

ERROR	CORRECTION

3. You think about past problems hitting out of bunkers, doubting your ability, then miss shots on the course that you hit well in practice.

3. Use thought stoppage; say, "I have done this 50 times in practice, and I know I can do it now."

Drills for Mental Preparation

1. Game of 5s Drill

Imagine that the range of tension possible in different body parts ranges from 1 to 5, with 3 being perfect for you. Systematically vary the tension in your shoulders, hands (grip), back, legs. For example, set the tension in your grip at 1 and hit 2 shots, then switch to a 5 and hit 2 shots.

Hit two shots at each tension level, (1, 5, 3) in each isolated body part, while maintaining an optimal 3 in all other body parts. Notice what hapens to the ball flight for each change in tension.

Success Goal = 24 total shots, varying tension

6 shots with shoulder tension: 2 shots at each level (1, 5, and 3)

6 shots with grip tension: 2 shots at each level (1, 5, and 3)

6 shots with tension in back: 2 shots at each level (1, 5, and 3)

6 shots with tension in legs: 2 shots at each level (1, 5, and 3)

Your Score =

(#) _____ shots, shoulder tension

(#) _____ shots, grip tension

(#) _____ shots, back tension

(#) _____ shots, leg tension

2. *Distraction Drill*

Actively distract your own attention while you attempt to hit golf balls. For example, hit while counting backward from 100 by 3s (i.e., 100, 97, 94, 91, . . .), reciting the alphabet backward, naming all of the students in your class, and so on. Notice what happens to your golf swing and the resultant ball flight.

Success Goal = 8 total shots, 6 of them with distractions

2 balls hit while counting backward by 3s

2 balls hit while reciting the alphabet backward

2 balls hit while naming everyone in class

2 balls hit with no distractions but using routine, relaxing, and using a swing cue

Your Score =

(#) _____ balls hit while counting backward by 3s

(#) _____ balls hit while reciting the alphabet backward

(#) _____ balls hit while naming everyone in class

(#) _____ balls hit while using your best routine

3. Possibilities Drill

While standing on the practice tee, imagine an actual hole from a golf course. State a self-doubting thought, STOP, use thought stoppage to replace the thought with a good one related to safe landing areas, and then execute your routine.

Success Goal =

   a. Imagine a large water hazard and a negative thought about your ability to hit over it. Stop this thought, replace it with a good thought, then hit a ball over the imaginary water.

   b. Imagine landing next to a sand trap and being afraid that your next shot would land in it. Stop this thought, replace it with a good one, and hit a ball over the imaginary trap.

   c. Imagine hitting a ball out-of-bounds and having to play a provisional ball from the same spot. Tell yourself that you can ''never make this shot.'' Stop this thought, replace it with a positive thought, and hit a ball in play.

   d. Make up your own negative situation and practice positive thoughts about it.

Your Score =

   a. _____ Check if you had a positive thought about the water hazard and hit a good shot over it.

   b. _____ Check if you had a positive thought about the sand trap and hit a good shot over it.

   c. _____ Check if you had a positive thought after hitting a ball out-of-bounds.

   d. _____ Write down the negative thought and the positive replacement thought that you chose.

Mental Skills
Keys to Success Checklist

When preparing for a round of golf, you must be aware of both your mental and physical skills. Using the following checklist, analyze the elements that may affect your golf skills.

Respond to each statement in terms of whether you strongly agree (SA), agree (A), disagree (D), or strongly disagree (SD) with it.

1. When I play golf, I have a great deal of tension in my

    a. neck and shoulders   SA   A   D   SD

    b. hands (grip)   SA   A   D   SD

    c. back   SA   A   D   SD

    d. legs   SA   A   D   SD

2. I use my preshot routine before each shot.   SA   A   D   SD

3. I have a specific cue to regain attention when I approach my next shot.   SA   A   D   SD

4. I always take my grip on the club from the same relative spot.   SA   A   D   SD

5. I use an intermediate target to aid in alignment.   SA   A   D   SD

6. I always align the clubface with the target line.   SA   A   D   SD

7. I can relax and reestablish tension control if I detect too much or too little tension.   SA   A   D   SD

8. After I hit a shot, I take time to remember how it felt and learn from it.   SA   A   D   SD

Step 13 Course Etiquette

Golf is a game that requires not only physical skills and mental concentration but also the proper social skills and etiquette for you to be welcomed on the course. Just like many other sports, there are certain unwritten rules of the game that signal others that you really know what is going on. This step describes the basic concepts of course etiquette and the social rules of the game.

WHY IS ETIQUETTE IMPORTANT?

Golf is often referred to as a game for gentlemen (and -women). When you play golf, you are expected to be courteous and to play by the rules. You are expected to make rule interpretations and call stroke penalties on yourself. You are also expected to treat your playing partners and the course with respect and commitment.

HOW TO DEMONSTRATE PROPER ETIQUETTE ON THE GOLF COURSE

Good golfers not only play honestly, but they respect their opponents and respect the game. For example, if you hit a shot into the woods, you must either find it or take a penalty; if the ball moves out of position when you address it, you must add a penalty stroke to your score. You are your own official. In contrast, how often have you seen a team sport player admitting to an umpire or referee that he or she accidently stepped out-of-bounds or fouled a net?

The rules of golf are carefully set down by the United States Golf Association (USGA) and the Royal and Ancient Golf Club of St. Andrews (R & A, the organization that governs golf in Great Britain). These rules are not intended to limit your play or enjoyment, but rather to guarantee it by selecting the rules that are the fairest to all players and to the integrity of the game.

In addition to these rules, there are also unofficial rules of etiquette that are designed to maximize the enjoyment of golf for everyone. The following tips to good golf etiquette summarize several courtesies that are generally expected on the golf course.

TEN KEYS TO SUCCESSFUL GOLF ETIQUETTE

There are ten areas in which you are expected to demonstrate appropriate social behavior. These include playing in groups, teeing off, understanding the order of play, behavior on greens, playing without delay, safety, course care, use of carts, appropriate dress, and being courteous to fellow golfers.

1. Playing in Groups

The game of golf is generally played with one to four persons in a group. It is, of course, possible to play by yourself, but generally people play in groups of up to four golfers. Because golf has become such a popular game, some golf courses require that you play in foursomes in order to make the course available to the greatest number of golfers. At such courses, you may be asked to play with other golfers of differing abilities. Fortunately, the handicapping system helps to make it fun to play with persons of many different abilities. Also, knowing the acceptable rules of etiquette helps your enjoyment when playing with new friends.

2. Teeing Off

When you want to play a round of golf, you are generally assigned a tee time. This is the time you and your partners are scheduled to hit your first ball and begin playing the round. If you are playing a course for the first time you may want to call to find out whether you need to reserve a specific tee time or whether you will be given a tee time upon arrival at the course. This means arriving at the course with enough time to spare so that you can warm up, hit some balls from the practice tee or putt some on the practice green, and still be ready to tee off at the designated time. If you are not there on time, you might not be allowed to play at all.

**Tee Off
on Time**

1. Make reservation for tee time.
2. Warm up ahead of time: Do your warm-up routine (stretching), hit balls on practice tee, practice on putting green.
3. Tee off on time (first person hits at designated time).

The first person to hit on the tee is said to ''have the honors.'' On the first hole, the honors are determined by a flip of the coin. For each hole after that, honors are given to the person with the lowest score on the previous hole. If two people scored the same, the honors remain with the person who had them on the previous hole, or if neither of the tied golfers had the last honors, their previous order of hitting remains in effect.

3. Order of Play on Fairway

Once all golfers have teed off, the golfer with the farthest distance yet to go to the green plays the next shot. All other golfers should wait behind an imaginary line through this golfer's ball so that safe golf can continue. Once the golfer has hit the ball, all golfers walk on toward their own balls or to the green, but not closer than the next golfer to hit.

**Order of Play
on Fairway**

1. Golfer farthest away from hole hits first.
2. All others stay behind hitter.
3. Everyone walks on toward own ball.

4. Behavior on the Green

On the green there are several points of etiquette that are important. You should be aware of the order of putting, the rules and courtesy associated with the flag, and the importance of moving off the green quickly when you have finished putting.

Once all players are on the putting green, the player who is farthest away from the hole putts first (this is referred to as being *away*, and is the same general type of rule as on the fairway). If some golfers are near the green but not yet on it, they should play onto the green before anyone putts. For example, even if your ball is on the green and 25 feet from the pin, if another player is 10 feet away but in the bunker, you may ask if he or she wants to hit before you putt.

If you are on the green and one of your playing partners has a long putt, it is a courtesy to *tend the flag*. By standing with one hand on the flag, you can see the hole clearly and can remove the flag as soon as the ball is stroked (putted) to avoid a possible penalty (if a putted ball hits an unattended flag, there is a 2-stroke penalty). Remember, if the ball is not on the green, it is all right to leave the flag in the hole. You should therefore always ask your partners whether they wish you to tend the flag. If you pull the flag, gently lay it down on the green or the fringe clearly out of the way of any stray putts.

**Order of Play
on Green**

1. All on green first.
2. Longest putt next.

**Tending
Flag**

1. Pull flag to putt if on green.
2. Lay flag out of way.
3. Ask partner to tend flag.
4. If ball is on fringe, leave flag in hole.

Putting greens are generally well groomed and watered often. Because of this careful care, they may be relatively soft. When you walk on a green, you may leave subtle footprints. It is therefore important never to take a step in the line of another person's putt. That is, you can see the line someone's ball will roll along toward the hole; do not step on or near this line.

5. Playing Without Delay

Nothing is more irritating to other golfers than slow players. This does not mean that you must rush your shots, but please make an effort to play with deliberate speed. Always be ready to hit when your turn comes. If you are waiting for another player to hit, be thinking about your shot, select your club, and prepare to swing. Once it is your turn, use your routine, get set, and swing smoothly.

You should do as much preparation before your turn as is possible. Just be careful not to distract your playing partners. Take your time in selecting the shot, but try to do it before it is literally your turn. Walk quickly between shots so that you have more time during your turn.

Once you have completed a hole, leave the green quickly and walk to the next tee. Then record your score and comment about your putts or chat momentarily if you wish. Never stay on the green and talk, or you may delay the group behind you when they should be hitting their approach shots.

If a single golfer or group of golfers behind you is catching up to you and is having to wait continuously before playing their shots, you should let the faster group "play through" if there is room in front of you. *Playing through* means that the players behind you pass you during the course of play. Allowing others to play through is a very important courtesy on the golf course. For example, if your ball goes out-of-bounds and you have to take time to search for it, check to see whether another group should be "waved through." Once you have signaled this group, be sure that you and your partners stay to the side of the course so that the others can safely play through.

Rapid Play

1. Watch behind you.
2. Walk quickly between shots.
3. Leave greens quickly.
4. Record score on next tee.

Others Playing Through

1. Check before hitting.
2. Allow rapid players to go ahead.
3. Signal it's safe to hit to golfers approaching behind you.

6. Always Be Aware of Safety

Golf is generally considered to be a very safe sport. However, it is played with two potentially dangerous "weapons": the club and the ball. A golf ball can be a deadly weapon if it strikes someone. One of the most vivid examples of the power of the clubbed ball is often demonstrated by "trick shot artists" who can set a piece of 1-inch thick plywood in front of a teed-up ball. When a good drive is executed, the ball goes through the piece of plywood!

Never hit a golf ball until you have checked to see that you have plenty of room to swing your club safely and that the other players on the course are well out of range. If ever in doubt, wait to hit. If you happen to hit a ball toward another golfer, yell "FORE!" as loud as you can. This is a universal warning signal for golfers and should result in the other golfers ducking or taking cover. Also, when letting a group play through, be sure to watch them hit, so you know where their balls are going.

Safety Tips

1. Check for clearance to swing.
2. Be sure no one is within range.
3. Hit only when safe.
4. Yell "FORE" if your ball may be dangerous to others.

7. Take Care of the Golf Course

The golf course is your playing field. You would not mistreat a basketball hardwood floor or wear your spikes on a clay tennis court—nor should you mistreat the golf course. For example, never drive or pull a golf cart onto a green or tee box. Similarly, be careful where and how you set down a flag if you pull it from the hole.

Replace All Divots: When you hit the fairway and take a "divot," or clump of grass, with your swing, stop to replace it. Pick up the divot, return it to the bare space, and gently step on it. Remember, you would not like to land in such a bare spot, so fix divots for the next golfer.

Rake All Bunkers: When you hit from a sand trap, be sure to rake it smooth before you leave it. Because you will need to rake it, it is usually smarter to enter the bunker from the shortest distance to the ball. When raking it, walk backward out of the bunker so that you can rake your footprints smooth as you leave the bunker. After you are finished with the rake, place the rake in a safe area with the spikes facing down.

Repair Ball Marks: Sometimes your ball leaves an indentation when it lands on the green from a great height or distance. If everyone left such marks on the green, it would look dimpled like a golf ball. You should repair these ball marks by inserting a tee under the depression at an angle and pressing down on it so that its tip elevates the turf to a normal level. Then gently tap down on the former depression with your putter. If you repair all of your ball marks and even others you come upon, the greens will be much smoother and easier to putt for everyone.

Replace Divots

1. Pick up divot (grass).
2. Replace in bare spot.
3. Step on grass.

Rake All Bunkers

1. Rake bunker smooth.
2. Leave no footprints.
3. Store rake safely.

Repair Ball Marks

1. Identify ball mark.
2. Insert tee under dent.
3. Press down on tee to raise earth.
4. Gently tap down.

8. Use of Carts

Many golfers prefer to wheel their golf bags on carts or to utilize motorized riding carts. Such carts are only optional conveniences for golfers and should be carefully located so as not to hurt the grass of the golf course. For example, never wheel a cart onto a green or across a hazard. When approaching the green, walk or ride around the green to the side near the next tee; park your cart there. Then, after you have putted, you can replace your putter in the bag and be ready to go briskly to the next tee.

Some golf courses have specific paths for motorized carts. It is essential that you follow these paths and, if the rules of the course require it, stay on the path at all times. If you are sharing a cart with another golfer, drive it to a location near the position from which you or your partner should hit the next shot. Park the cart and either stay with it or walk a short distance to your shot. Then drive on together.

9. Dress for Success

Many golf courses require appropriate clothing. In general, slacks, golf skirts, or midthigh shorts are appropriate, but some courses do not allow short-shorts or running shorts. Some courses also require collared shirts and do not permit T-shirts or tank tops. The best rule of thumb is to dress conservatively and neatly.

You must wear golf shoes or smooth-soled shoes (like tennis shoes) in order to protect the golf course. It is never appropriate to wear street shoes or shoes with heavy treads or heels.

10. Treat All Players With Courtesy

When playing golf, it is courteous to be quiet and not move while others are hitting or putting. By not disturbing other players, you help them play their best, and they will help you, too.

When someone is about to strike a golf ball, be sure that you are not in his or her line of sight. This generally means staying to the side or behind so that you cannot be seen even in his or her peripheral vision. You must also be careful not to allow your shadow to cross the path of another's putt (see Figure 13.1). This is a more subtle distractor, but being aware of it is a very powerful indicator to others that you really are a true golfer.

Figure 13.1 Do not allow your shadow to cross the path of another's putt.

If you treat all players with courtesy and fairness, they will treat you with the same respect. Remember, it is only fun to play the game when everyone plays under the same conditions. Treat others the way you would like to be treated.

Step 14 Shot Selection and Course Management

In this step you learn about course management, your strategy for playing each hole. In Steps 3 through 9, you developed the component skills necessary to play golf. Now it is time to put these skills together and learn how to score. Course management has to do with applying these skills in a variety of situations to go from the tee to the green in the fewest number of strokes. This step helps you develop your game strategy, using a three-step approach: (a) assess, (b) identify, and (c) plot.

WHY IS COURSE MANAGEMENT IMPORTANT?

Can you imagine a coach preparing for a game without a game plan? Just as a coach matches the players' strengths against the weaknesses of the other team, you must match up your skills with the golf course's characteristics. Your ability to analyze the strengths and weaknesses of a hole, along with the knowledge of your current ability, helps you to develop a strategy for playing the holes and selecting your routes to the greens. Course management allows you to match your strengths as a player against the weaknesses of a hole. This is "percentage golf" and is important in your becoming a consistent player. Course management puts you in control of your game.

HOW TO SELECT SHOTS AND MANAGE THE COURSE

Course management is the real challenge in golf. Many golfers are good practice players because there are no consequences. The conditions in practice remain the same, and it is easy not to have to make many decisions. To become a good player, though, you must learn to think yourself around the course. You must assess your current strengths and weaknesses as a player, identify the strengths and weaknesses of the specific golf hole you are about to play, and choose the best strategy, given these considerations, in planning a route to the green.

The first step in course management is to *assess* your own strengths and weaknesses as a player. When you practice and play, use the drills that were presented with each step to help you in this assessment. How close do you come to the Success Goals? When you use the charts to record your ball flights, do you have any biases in your shots? For example, do you tend to hit more balls to the right or left of your target with your irons or woods? Do you tend to hit more chip shots long, short, or on-target? Step 10 provided a systematic way to practice, which is the key to developing awareness of your strengths and weaknesses.

The second step is to *identify* the strengths and weaknesses of each hole. The tough things about a hole are referred to as the hole's *strengths*. Strengths include such things as the hazards (water and sand), out-of-bounds areas, small fairways and greens, and high roughs. Most holes have specific strengths that were designed to give the golfer trouble. On the other hand, there are weaknesses in most holes, which should tell you where to aim. For example, find the widest part of the fairway, aim away from the hazards, look for an opening to the green where there are no traps, find the largest part of the green to aim at rather than always aiming at the flag (see Figure 14.1).

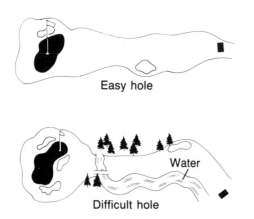

Figure 14.1 Potential trouble areas determine the strengths and weaknesses of a hole.

The identification of a hole's strengths and weaknesses can often take place from the tee. Carefully look at the entire hole. Where are the weaknesses of the hole? Where are the strengths? Are there any distinguishable yardage markers? For some holes, you may not be able to see the entire hole from the tee. Often the scorecard has a printed layout of the course with yardage marked, or one of your playing partners may be familiar with the course. If you are going to play in a tournament, you should try to play a pretournament round in order to become familiar with the course.

The third step is to compare your strengths to the weaknesses of the hole and *plot* a path

to the green. For example, standing on the tee, you should first look at both the strengths and weaknesses of the hole. If you see a sand trap on the right side, you probably want to select a landing area on the left side of the fairway. By determining a good strategy, you avoid the trouble built into the course and take advantage of the good landing areas (see Figure 14.2).

Once you have planned your strategy for the hole, you can then select the appropriate club for each shot. This selection is based on the position or lie of the ball, the trajectory of the shot, and the desired distance to your target or landing area. Each of these aspects is important to the golfer, and are sometimes referred to as the *LTD process*: the *lie* of the ball, the needed *trajectory*, and the desired *distance*. The lie of the ball is determined by its position in the sand, grass, or on a bare spot or divot. For example, if in the sand, is the ball sitting on top of the sand or buried? In the fairway, is the ball on top of the grass or resting in a divot? The lie can also be influenced by the height or texture of the grass.

Ideal shot trajectory is a matter of how high or low you wish to hit the shot. Is the normal trajectory for a particular club adequate? Are there any trees or shrubs to go over?

The distance is determined by how far you wish to hit the next shot. It is important to remember that it is not always necessary to hit the ball as far as you possibly can. Sometimes you wish to hit it a controlled, shorter distance in order to be in a good position to hit your next shot. For example, if there is a water hazard in front of the green and you are 180 yards away, you may wish to hit short of the water and then hit your third shot onto the green.

Your club selection ultimately must depend on all three elements of *LTD*—lie, trajectory, and distance. For example, a wood is not recommended from high grass, yet the distance might naturally call for that club. In such a case, a mid-iron might become the preferred club because of the grassy conditions.

Figure 14.2 Keys to
Successful Course
Management:
Analyzing
Strengths and
Weaknesses

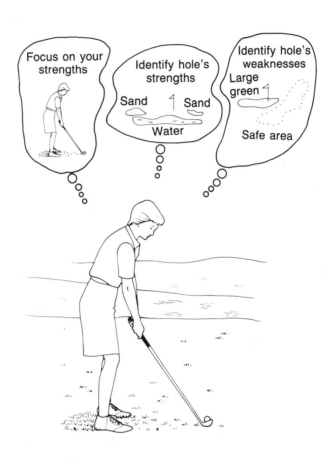

Your
Strengths

1. Control of ball direction
2. Ball trajectory per club
3. Distance hit per club

4. Consistent ball curvature
5. Psychological charac-
   teristics

Hole's Strengths

1. Hazards (water/sand)
2. Out-of-bounds
3. Tight fairway
4. Small green
5. Narrow opening to green
6. High rough
7. Trees and shrubs

Hole's Weaknesses

1. Minimal hazards
2. No out-of-bounds
3. Wide fairway
4. Large green
5. Big opening to green (no traps)
6. Close-cut rough
7. Safe landing areas

Detecting Errors in Course Management

Many of the problems in shot selection and course management come from not taking the time to make good decisions. Outstanding golfers allow themselves time to analyze the situation and match each hole's demands with their skills.

ERROR

CORRECTION

1. Ball generally lands short of green when you use 4-iron.

2. Tee shots usually miss fairway when you use 3-wood.

1. Take "one more club" than you think; that is, if you believe you should hit with a 4-iron, choose a 5-wood or 3-iron.

2. Tee off with 5-wood or long iron.

ERROR   **CORRECTION**

3. When you try to hook ball around dogleg, ball winds up in woods.

3. Play for middle of fairway, particularly if you tend to slice.

4. When there is lateral water hazard on hole, ball always seems to land there.

4. Use tension control to feel level 3 grip. Be sure to use routine and focus on the good landing areas rather than being distracted by water.

Course Management Drills

1. *Imaginary Hole*

It is important to be able to match your strengths and weaknesses with those of a golf hole. To begin practicing this skill, imagine that you are on the first tee of a golf course, though you're actually on a practice tee. Determine the desired landing area in an open space. Use the obstacles or flags in the field to represent "trouble" on the hole. Select the safe landing areas and then actually hit a shot toward each one.

Success Goal = choose 10 different safe landing areas, hit 1 ball to each target area, and have balls land in safe areas 8 of 10 times

Your Score =

Shot	Landing area	Club used	Fate of ball
Example	Between blue flag and orange cone	5-iron	Good shot, slightly long
1			
2			
3			
4			
5			
6			
7			
8			
9			
10			

2. Alternate Strategies

In your mind create an imaginary hole. Imagine that each obstacle in your practice field is a hazard or trouble spot on a real hole. For example, pretend that the area between two flags or cones is really a lake. Find a landing area away from that "water hazard."

Pretend you are three different golfers, with different characteristic strengths and weaknesses. As each golfer, determine a different strategy for playing the hole. Identify the safe landing area, and choose the club to be used for your first shot. As golfer #1, assume that you are a long hitter with a good short game. What landing area would you choose, and what club would you hit? As golfer #2, assume that you hit short and tend to slice the ball. Golfer #3 is really you. Describe yourself and determine your preferred route.

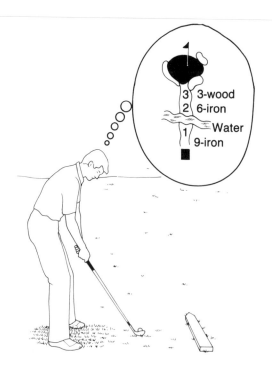

Success Goal = select a route for each type of golfer, specify the club used, and hit the shot

1. Long hitter with good short game
2. Short hitter who tends to slice
3. You

Your Score = diagram the selected landing area, route, and actual outcome

As golfer #1   *As golfer #2*   *As golfer #3*

3. Listing Strengths and Weaknesses

Given the sample of three golf holes below, identify the strengths and weaknesses of the holes. Write a brief description of each and mark their locations on the diagram. Mark each hole's strengths as s1, s2 and s3; indicate the locations of the weaknesses as w1, w2, w3 (see example hole).

Example hole

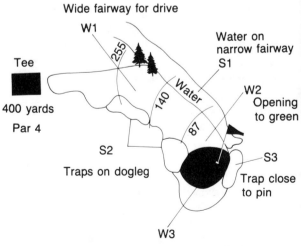

Wide fairway for drive

W1

255

Water on narrow fairway
S1

Tee

140 Water

W2
Opening to green

400 yards

Par 4

87

S2

Traps on dogleg

S3

Trap close to pin

W3

Big green to side of pin

Success Goal = listing at least three strengths and three weaknesses for each hole

Your Score =

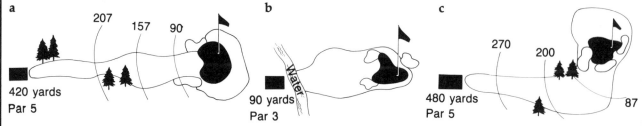

a
207 157 90
420 yards
Par 5

b
Water
90 yards
Par 3

c
270 200
480 yards
Par 5
87

Hole's strengths (a)	Hole's strengths (b)	Hole's strengths (c)
s1. _____	s1. _____	s1. _____
s2. _____	s2. _____	s2. _____
s3. _____	s3. _____	s3. _____

Hole's weaknesses (a)	Hole's weaknesses (b)	Hole's weaknesses (c)
w1. _____	w1. _____	w1. _____
w2. _____	w2. _____	w2. _____
w3. _____	w3. _____	w3. _____

4. Managing an Entire Hole

When you decide to plot a strategy for a given hole, you must match your strengths as a golfer with the weaknesses of the hole. Identify your preferred landing area for each shot by marking an X over the spot. Indicate the club you should use to hit the ball from that location by placing a symbol adjacent to the X (e.g., 4i = 4-iron; 3w = 3-wood; pw = pitching wedge). See the example hole below.

Example hole

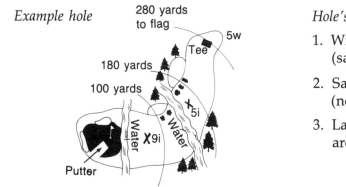

280 yards to flag
5w
Tee
180 yards
100 yards
Water
X 5i
Water
X 9i
Putter

Hole's weaknesses

1. Wide landing area off tee (safe area along left)

2. Safe area in front of water (no hazards)

3. Large green (good landing area beyond flag)

Clubs to use

5w
5i
9i
putter

Success Goal = identify each hole's weaknesses, plot all shots for each hole, and indicate the clubs to use

Your Score =

a

170 yards

341 yards

Par 4

Sand

b

168 yards

Par 4

Water

c

502 yards

Par 5

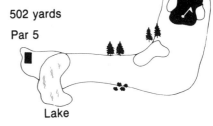

Lake

Hole's weaknesses (a)	Hole's weaknesses (b)	Hole's weaknesses (c)
1. _____	1. _____	1. _____
2. _____	2. _____	2. _____
3. _____	3. _____	3. _____

Clubs to use (list in order and plot on the diagram)   Clubs to use (list in order and plot on the diagram)   Clubs to use (list in order and plot on the diagram)

5. Managing a Round

Ultimately, the task in golf is to plot your strategy for a round of golf. Given an entire 18-hole course layout, determine how you would ideally play each hole, given your strengths and weaknesses. Lay out the shots you would make on each hole. Mark an **X** on the landing area and indicate the *club* you should hit from each location.

Success Goal = plot your course management for each of 18 holes

Your Score =

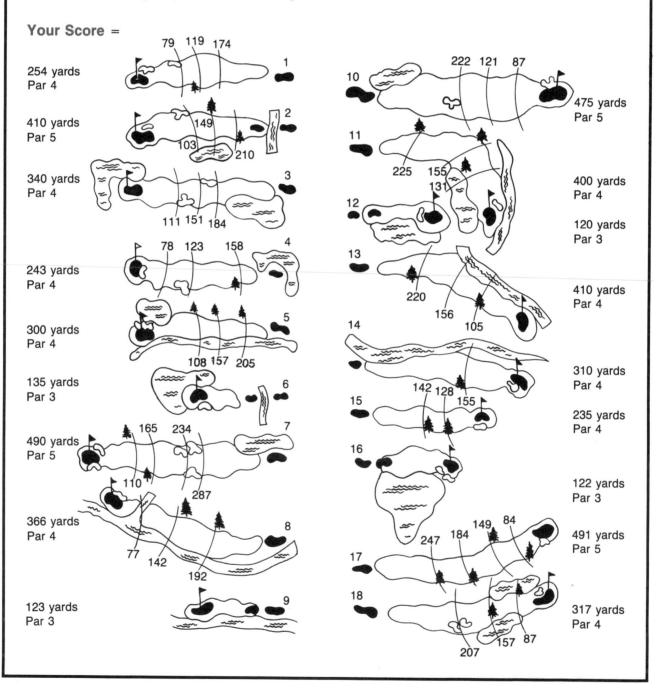

254 yards
Par 4

410 yards
Par 5

340 yards
Par 4

243 yards
Par 4

300 yards
Par 4

135 yards
Par 3

490 yards
Par 5

366 yards
Par 4

123 yards
Par 3

475 yards
Par 5

400 yards
Par 4

120 yards
Par 3

410 yards
Par 4

310 yards
Par 4

235 yards
Par 4

122 yards
Par 3

491 yards
Par 5

317 yards
Par 4

Course Management
Keys to Success Checklist

In determining your ability to match your skills (strengths) against the weaknesses of a golf hole, you may wish to refer to this checklist. Place a check on the line for each element you consider when you attempt to determine your strategy for each hole.

Preparation
Phase

Analyzing Your Own
Strengths

_____ Distance you hit each club

_____ Any biases regarding shot direction (push, straight, pull)

_____ Any biases regarding curvature of shots (slices or hooks)

_____ Typical shot trajectory with each club

Psychological characteristics

_____ Concern for hazards rather than landing areas

_____ Tension

_____ Attentional control

Execution
Phase

Selecting a Route

_____ Locate safe landing areas, as opposed to hazards or other trouble

_____ Locate out-of-bounds areas

_____ Consider width of fairway as narrow (tight) or wide (open)

_____ Find opening to green (free of hazards)

_____ Consider location and height of rough

Selecting a Club

_____ Lie of ball

_____ Trajectory of desired shot

_____ Distance ball must travel

**Follow-Up
Phase**

**Keeping Track
of Performance**

____ Review decisions regarding hole's weaknesses

____ Review decisions regarding selecting route

____ Review decisions regarding selection of club

____ Make mental note for future reference

Step 15   Learning From Your Round of Golf

Whenever you hit a golf ball, you can learn something about your swing. In Step 4, we discussed learning to watch the flight of your ball in order to identify your strengths and to detect basic problems with your golf swing. This technique can help you on the practice tee and the course, but you need other skills to help detect your strengths and weaknesses from a regulation round of golf.

When you play golf, you almost never use the same club twice in a row. Because of the constant demands to match the requirements of shots, it is easy to lose track of just how well you are doing. In this step, you learn several techniques to help you systematically identify your strengths and weaknesses during a round of golf.

WHY IS LEARNING FROM YOUR ROUND OF GOLF IMPORTANT?

Some golfers are very good practice players and seem to hit many excellent shots in practice, but do not play well when they attempt an actual round of golf. The round of golf should be used just like practice for you to learn more about yourself and your golf game. By focusing on what you have done and what you thought or felt, you learn more about your skills. Use the information from the round to analyze the mental and physical aspects of your game.

HOW TO LEARN FROM A ROUND OF GOLF

During your golf play, you should try to hit your best shot each time you strike a ball. When you hit a good shot, try to remember how you prepared to hit it and how it felt during the swing. Of course, it is not always possible to hit great shots, so it is also important to try to determine what went wrong when you mis-hit a ball. Pay attention to your mental preparation to hit the ball and to the physical aspects of your swing.

In golf the competitive situation involves an actual round of golf in which you can test your skills and abilities. During a round, you may use every club in your bag and hit 100 or more shots. This experience should give you a wealth of information about your golf skills, if you are systematic about keeping track of your performance. It is important to pay attention to how well you execute each swing. Just like a basketball player might keep track of the position on the floor from which he or she shot, you should keep track of the golf clubs and shots you used. This tracking system should include both the physical outcome of your swings and your psychological characteristics and control during the round.

After each shot, try to remember what happened to the ball. Determine what might have caused any problems. *What were the physical characteristics of the shot*? What was the ball flight? Was it on line with the target? Was there excessive curve in the ball flight (a slice or hook)? What was the trajectory? Was the distance the shot traveled about right for that particular club? Were there problems with alignment, the path of the swing (causing a push or pull), topping or popping up the ball, or selecting a club—problems that resulted in a shot that was too short or too long in relation to the desired target?

Shot Mapping

One excellent way to learn from a round of golf is to keep track of each shot you hit. By actually drawing each golf hole, it is easy to record the shots that you hit. This *shot mapping* technique is a very convenient way to be able to remember what shots you took and how well you executed them. Figure 15.1 illustrates a chart of 9 holes of golf. Notice that for each hole, the club that was used as well as a note about the results are recorded.

Figure 15.1   Keys to Success: Learning From a Round

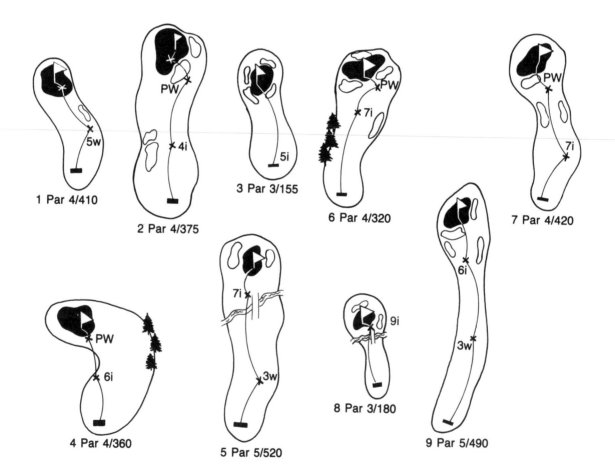

Observe and Record
Physical Skills

1. Alignment of feet and body
2. Path of swing: push or pull ball

3. Face of club at impact: slice or hook
4. Club selection
5. Distance ball traveled

Sense and Record
Mental Skills

1. Preshot routine
2. Attention control

3. Positive self-talk
4. Tension control

Shotkeeper Scorecard

The result of each golf ball you hit is affected by two shot aspects: your physical swing and your mental state when you hit the ball. The errors or strengths that result from psychological skills are not as easy to detect as physical skills. You cannot see them, and no one else can see them to tell you about them. You must be the detective; be sensitive to your own body and mind and determine what happened. When you hit the last shot, were you tense, distracted, rushed, unable to concentrate? Record any of these feelings so that you can practice good mental skills just like you practice the physical aspects of your game.

Another good way to learn from your round of golf is to use a simple scorecard to record each shot taken. This allows you to systematically collect data on each of the clubs in your bag and on your mental and physical skills. For example, the Shotkeeper Scorecard is a simple device to record each shot (see Figure 15.2). Simply record two items for each club used: notations about the physical results of the shot and the mental skills you demonstrated.

In the Sample Shotkeeper Scorecard that Tony completed, notice the tendencies tallied on the scoresheet (see Figure 15.3). There were 9 slices, compared to only 1 hook. There were also 23 instances of having excess body tension, whereas only once was underarousal a problem. From this simple example it is easy to see that one problem for Tony may be tension, preventing the return of the clubface to a square position at impact. This tendency to be too aroused often causes an open clubface, which results in slicing the ball.

Figure 15.2 Shotkeeper Scorecard

Name _____   Course _____   Date _____

Performance Chart

Hole	Yards	PAR	Woods					Irons									Wedge	Greens hit in Regulation	Putts		
			1	2	3	4	5	1	2	3	4	5	6	7	8	9			1st	2nd	3rd
1																						
2																						
3																						
4																						
5																						
6																						
7																						
8																						
9																						
10																						
11																						
12																						
13																						
14																						
15																						
16																						
17																						
18																						

Physical Aspects
✔ = on target
s = sliced
h = hooked
o = beyond target
u = short of target
r = right of target
l = left of target

Mental Aspects
NT = Negative Thinking
LA = Lack of Attentional Control
BT = Excess Body Tension
FR = Failure to use Routine
OA = Overaroused
UA = Underaroused
CC = Complete Mental Control

Summary: **Physical Aspects**

✔ =   o =
s =   u =
h =   r =
           l =

Mental Aspects

NT =   OA =
LA =   UA =
BT =   CC=
FR =

Figure 15.3 Sample Shotkeeper Scorecard

Name Tony Jones   Course Richmont CC   Date Sept. 9

Performance Chart

Hole	Yards	PAR	Woods 1	Woods 2	Woods 3	Woods 4	Woods 5	Irons 1	Irons 2	Irons 3	Irons 4	Irons 5	Irons 6	Irons 7	Irons 8	Irons 9	Wedge	Greens hit in Regulation	Putts 1st	Putts 2nd	Putts 3rd
1	385	4			S BT							S BT					L BT		u CC	✓ CC	✓ CC
2	142	3												S BT			✓ CC		o FR	u FR	✓ CC
3	501	5			R FR		✓ CC				R FR	L FR				✓ FR	✓ FR		u BT	✓ CC	✓ CC
4	365	4			S BT		R FR									✓ FR			u BT	o FR	✓ CC
5	325	4					R FR					✓				L FR	✓ FR		u BT	✓ CC	✓ BT
6	129	3					h FR					L FR		o FR		L FR	✓ FR	✓	u BT	✓ FR	✓ BT
7	498	5			S BT		h FR					L FR		o FR		L FR			✓ BT	✓ BT	✓ BT
8	301	4					✓ FR					S BT		L FR		L FR	✓ CC		u FR	✓ BT	✓ BT
9	379	4					✓ CC					R FR		L FR		L FR	✓ CC		o CC	✓ CC	u FR
10	516	5			S BT		✓ CC				R FR	R FR		L FR			✓ BT		u FR	✓ FR	✓ BT
11	329	4			S BT		✓ CC					R FR					✓ BT		✓ BT	✓ CC	✓ CC
12	145	3									R FR								✓ CC	✓ FR	u FR
13	371	4					✓ CC					L FR				L FR	✓ BT		o FR	✓ CC	✓ BT
14	298	4			R FR		✓ CC					R FR				u FR	✓ CC		o FR	✓ CC	✓ CC
15	520	5					✓ CC					R FR				u FR	✓ CC		✓ FR	✓ CC	u FR
16	318	4			S BT							R FR				u FR	✓ CC	✓	u FR	✓ CC	u FR
17	141	3									✓ CC								✓ FR	✓ CC	✓ CC
18	352	4					✓ UA					R BT				u FR	o FR		u FR	✓ FR	✓ CC

Physical Aspects

✓ = on target
s = sliced
h = hooked
o = beyond target
u = short of target
r = right of target
l = left of target

Mental Aspects

NT = Negative Thinking
LA = Lack of Attentional Control
BT = Excess Body Tension
FR = Failure to use Routine
OA = Overaroused
UA = Underaroused
CC = Complete Mental Control

Summary:

Physical Aspects		Mental Aspects	
✓ = 43	o = 8	NT = —	OA = —
s = 9	u = 12	LA = —	UA = 1
h = 1	r = 12	BT = 24	CC = 28
	l = 11	FR = 42	

Note. From *Golf: Better Practice for Better Play* by L. Bunker & D. Owens, 1984, p. 210. Copyright 1984 by Leisure Press. Adapted by permission.

Detecting Errors and Planning Practice

After completing the round, simply tally the columns to determine your major strengths and weaknesses. For example, look down the column of all the shots taken with your 5-iron and see the typical results. How many times did you hit the ball over the target, to the right or left, without using your routine? What was your mental control each time you hit the ball? These tallies should help you determine on what you should spend the majority of your practice time in the near future. They also help you learn to set goals in order to help with your continued success (see Step 16).

The Shotkeeper can also be an effective aid during practice. Keep track of the number and results of shots taken with each club. You may even wish to work with a partner so that each of you can use the Shotkeeper for the other golfer.

ERROR   **CORRECTION**

The following errors are taken from Figure 15.3 and illustrate some of Tony's typical problems.

1. 9-iron shots seem to fall short.	1. Select a 7-iron instead.
2. Golfer failed to use routine on 42 shots.	2. Practice using routine each time.
3. 3-wood drives tend to slice.	3. Practice tension control when using woods; allow hands to find tension level 3 and release through impact.
4. Most putting misses occur to right of hole.	4. Check alignment, eyes over ball and clubhead path square to target.
5. Most missed putts are accompanied by failure to use routine or by being overaroused.	5. Practice using preshot routine each time; be sure to monitor tension.

Shotkeeping Drills

1. Using Shotkeeper From Practice Tee

Using a Shotkeeper to record the results of each swing, play 6 holes of golf from the practice tee. For each hole, diagram and record the specific clubs used, the shot resulting from each swing, and the mental aspects that were present when you took the swing.

Success Goal = pretend that you are playing 6 holes, diagram them (see example holes), record each club used and physical and mental aspects of shots, then tally results in terms of characteristics

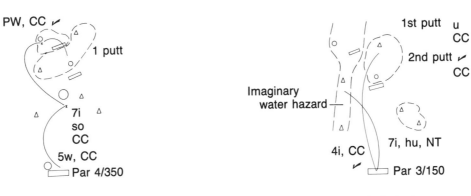

Example hole 1   *Example hole 2*

Hole 1   *Hole 2*   *Hole 3*

Hole 4   *Hole 5*   *Hole 6*

Shotkeeper Scorecard

Name _____ Course _____ Date _____

Performance Chart

Hole	Yards	PAR	Woods 1	2	3	4	5	Irons 1	2	3	4	5	6	7	8	9	Wedge	Greens hit in Regulation	Putts 1st	2nd	3rd
1																					
2																					
3																					
4																					
5																					
6																					
7																					
8																					
9																					
10																					
11																					
12																					
13																					
14																					
15																					
16																					
17																					
18																					

Physical Aspects
✓ = on target
s = sliced
h = hooked
o = beyond target
u = short of target
r = right of target
l = left of target

Mental Aspects
NT = Negative Thinking
LA = Lack of Attentional Control
BT = Excess Body Tension
FR = Failure to use Routine
OA = Overaroused
UA = Underaroused
CC = Complete Mental Control

Summary:

Physical Aspects		Mental Aspects	
✓ =	o =	NT =	OA =
s =	u =	LA =	UA =
h =	r =	BT =	CC =
	l =	FR =	

Your Score =

Physical Aspects

(#) _____ shots too long (o)

(#) _____ shots too short (u)

(#) _____ shots landing to right of target (r)

(#) _____ shots landing to left of target (l)

(#) _____ shots sliced (s)

(#) _____ shots hooked (h)

(#) _____ shots on target (✓)

Mental Aspects

(#) _____ negative thinking (NT)

(#) _____ lacked attentional control (LA)

(#) _____ excess body tension (BT)

(#) _____ failed to use routine (FR)

(#) _____ underaroused or too relaxed (UA)

(#) _____ complete mental control (CC)

2. Plotting Holes

Play at least 6 holes of golf and plot your shots and mental states on a diagram of the holes on a Shotkeeper.

Summarize your performance by tallying the results for each club used and the types of physical and mental behaviors. For example, how many times did you hit the ball to the right or left? How many times did you fail to utilize your routine?

Success Goal = note at least one mental and one physical aspect of each shot

Your Score = fill in Shotkeeper Scorecard and summarize aspects noted

Shotkeeper Scorecard

Name _____ Course _____ Date _____

Hole	Yards	PAR	Woods 1	2	3	4	5	Irons 1	2	3	4	5	6	7	8	9	Wedge	Greens hit in Regulation	Putts 1st	2nd	3rd
1																					
2																					
3																					
4																					
5																					
6																					
7																					
8																					
9																					
10																					
11																					
12																					
13																					
14																					
15																					
16																					
17																					
18																					

Performance Chart

Physical Aspects
✓ = on target
s = sliced
h = hooked
o = beyond target
u = short of target
r = right of target
l = left of target

Mental Aspects
NT = Negative Thinking
LA = Lack of Attentional Control
BT = Excess Body Tension
FR = Failure to use Routine
OA = Overaroused
UA = Underaroused
CC = Complete Mental Control

Summary: **Physical Aspects**   **Mental Aspects**

✓ =	o =	NT = OA =
s =	u =	LA = UA =
h =	r =	BT = CC=
	l =	FR =

3. Organizing Practice

Organize your practice based on the Shotkeeper results from the previous drill. List the skills you need to work on the most and decide how to practice them. For example, if you hit the majority of your shots off to the right of your target, make a commitment to practice at least 30 shots using the alignment drill (see Step 2, Drill 3).

Success Goal = select two aspects of game to practice, decide how to practice them, list them below, then do what you have prescribed

Your Score =

1. "I need to practice _____ . Therefore, I will do _____ drill _____ times." (You may list multiple drills.)

2. "I need to practice _____ . Therefore, I will do _____ drill _____ times." (You may list multiple drills.)

Learning From a Round of Golf
Keys to Success Checklist

You have been determining strengths and weaknesses for your golf skills by using the charting and Shotkeeper techniques. Summarize your tendencies for each category below.

**Physical
Aspects**

Tendency to be on target

____ distance

____ direction

Tendencies related to distance

____ beyond target more than 15 yards (o)

____ short of target more than 15 yards (u)

Tendencies related to path

____ push balls

____ pull balls

Tendencies related to clubface

____ slices (s) or

____ hooks (h)

Mental Aspects

____ Tendency to use negative thinking (NT)

____ Tendency to lack attentional control (LA)

____ Tendency to have excess body tension (BT)

____ Failure to use preshot routines (FR)

____ Tendency to be overaroused or too tense (OA)

____ Tendency to be underaroused or too relaxed (UA)

____ Tendency to have complete control (CC)

Step 16 Setting Goals for Continued Success

You have now reached the top of the staircase at last. You have made it through 15 other steps and have arrived at the 16th. As in any journey, though, it is not merely enough to get through each turn or each step: You must learn from each and be prepared to continue to learn.

Throughout the first 15 steps, you have measured your ability against the success goals presented for each drill. You have also determined the quality of your skills by having others watch you and give you feedback in terms of the Keys to Success Checklists. In addition, you have become skilled at learning from your practice and rounds of golf by using the Shotkeeper.

Once you have identified your strengths and weaknesses, it is time to set your own goals and establish your own criteria for improvement. Once you have determined these goals, you can plan your practice so that you continue to improve your golf skills.

WHY IS GOAL SETTING IMPORTANT?

In order to get the most out of practice, it is important to have predetermined objectives or goals. Goals help you maintain motivation, direct your attention, and determine whether you are getting better. Goals are therefore important for continued improvement and efficient practice.

HOW TO DETERMINE APPROPRIATE GOALS

The first phase of goal setting is to identify your strengths and weaknesses in terms of your objectives. For example, if you wish to have a 15 handicap by the end of the summer, you must make a commitment to serious practice, focusing on your major weaknesses. In order to accomplish this, there are three steps

to goal setting. Start by making a list of 4 or 5 long-term goals, for example, "I will improve my putting skills."

Your list of long-term goals focuses your attention, but it does not provide you with a detailed practice regimen. The next step is to make each of those goals more *specific* and *measurable*. By analyzing each long-term goal, you can establish specific short-term goals, such as the following:

- Hit 8 of 10 putts to within 1 foot of these distances: 3, 4, 5, 6, 7, 8, 9 feet.
- Hit 7 of 10 5-irons 125 yards (plus or minus 10 yards).
- Hit 6 of 10 shots with a 5-wood straight.
- Hit 8 of 10 pitches within 15 yards of the target.
- Hit 7 of 10 chip shots with a 9-iron over my golf bag to within 3 feet of the hole from 10, 15, and 20 yards away.

Notice that some of the goals have higher expectations than others—6 of 10, as compared to 8 of 10—based on your own particular skills. Each goal must be *achievable* within your own present skill level and the amount of time you want to practice.

It is also important to check that your goals are written in a positive, practice-directing fashion. State your goals in a way that focuses your attention on what you want to accomplish, not what you want to avoid. For example, you could have written a goal such as "Hook the ball no more than 3 of 10 times," but who knows—that might have caused you to slice it the rest of the time! Instead, state the goal like this: "Hit a straight ball 7 of 10 times."

Each goal statement should identify achievable and measurable skills; it should also set the expectation that you accomplish these skills within a certain amount of time. These *target dates* are not rigid deadlines, but they should be realistic lengths of time in which you can attain the specific goals. Your target dates should help you focus your attention and be consistent in your practice by reminding you of the urgency of accomplishing your goals.

The third step in effective goal setting is to design a practice strategy that helps you develop the skills necessary to meet your goals. Many of the practice techniques are easy to identify if you look back at the drills in each of the previous chapters. For example, practicing the Putting Ladder Drill or the Cluster Putting Drill (see Step 7) at least once per day for the next 10 days would be a good way to move toward accomplishing the first sample long-term goal above.

GOAL SETTING: KEYS TO SUCCESS

1. Determine your strengths and weaknesses (physical and mental) for each club by referring to checklists and Shotkeepers.

2. List four or five long-term goals.

3. Make each long-term goal more specific by stating it in measurable terms and specifying a time limit for achieving it.

4. Establish a practice strategy for each goal.

5. Focus attention on desirable, positive behavior.

Goal Setting Drills

1. Identifying Areas for Improvement Drill

To identify your areas for improvement, play 9 holes of golf and keep track of your shots with the Shotkeeper (see Appendix B). Make a list of your physical and mental weaknesses: Look for any tendencies that repeat (e.g., 70% of shots go to the right of the target).

Success Goal = selecting one element for improvement in each of the following categories: Woods, long irons, mid-irons, short irons, chipping, pitching, putting, sand play, and uneven lies

Your Score = identify improvement needed:

Woods _____

Long irons _____

Mid-irons _____

Short irons _____

Chipping _____

Pitching _____

Putting _____

Sand play _____

Uneven lies _____

2. *Goal Setting Drill*

In order to become a good practice golfer, you must be able to translate the weaknesses you have identified into specific goals, which then direct your practice.

Assume that you discovered the following things from your Shotkeeper:

a. 3 of 4 drives were sliced.
b. You failed to use routine 12 times.
c. 2 of 3 shots with 9-iron did not go high in the air.
d. 7 of 9 first putts were short of the hole.

State a goal for each observation. Be sure it is *specific, measurable,* and *time-constrained.*

Success Goal = write and evaluate four well-stated goals

Your Score = a specific (S), measurable (M), and time-constrained (T) goal statement for each of four areas needing improvement. Place a check under the column if it meets the criteria.

Improvement needed

a. _____

b. _____

c. _____

d. _____

	Goal statement	S	M	T
a.	_____	____	____	____
b.	_____	____	____	____
c.	_____	____	____	____
d.	_____	____	____	____

3. Future Improvement Identification Drill

In order to plan your strategy for future improvement, it is important to identify your strengths and weaknesses systematically.

Success Goal = using the Shotkeeper as a source of information to complete the future improvement targets card.

Your Score = complete future improvement targets card

Future Improvement Targets for Golf

Name _____   Date _____

For each of the clubs listed below, identify the typical characteristics you see in the ball flight coming from each kind of club. Use the same abbreviations used in the Shotkeeper Scorecard and describe each characteristic in terms of the number of times out of 10 that something happened, for example, Driver: 7 of 10 slices.

Woods: Driver 　　　　3– or 5–Wood
Long Irons: 1–3
Middle Irons: 4–6
Short Irons: 7–9
Pitching Wedge
Sand Wedge
Putting

4. Goal Achievement Card Drill

Using each of the characteristics identified as future improvement targets in Drill 1, write a specific goal for each element.

Each statement should be written as an achievable and measurable expectation with a specific target date.

Success Goal = identifying 5 specific goals and determining a practice strategy and target date for each

Your Score = complete goal achievement card

Goal Achievement Card

Name _____   Date _____

Skill	Specific Goal	Practice Strategy	Target Date
Example: Putting	Putt 7 of 10 balls into hole from 5 feet	Cluster Putting Drill 5 times Ladder Drill 5 times Line Drill 5 times	April 5
1. Long Irons or Woods			
2. Middle Irons			
3. Short Irons			
4. Chipping and Pitching			
5. Putting			

Goal Setting
Keys to Success Checklist

Having specific goals will not only help to direct your practice, they can also keep you motivated! As you plan your practice, be sure to analyze your strengths and weaknesses, and then write specific goals for yourself. The following checklist will help you check if your goals are effectively written.

Determine Targets
for Improvement

_____ Review each club

_____ Determine ball flight characteristics with each club

_____ Determine mental characteristics

Write Specific
Goals

_____ Achievable

_____ Stated positively

_____ Measurable

_____ Realistic time line

_____ Target dates established

Determine Practice
Strategies

_____ Specific to each goal

_____ Realistic

Rating Your Golf Progress

There are several success goals in learning golf. One is to develop an appreciation for the game and a desire to pursue it as a leisure activity. The second goal is to achieve a level of skill that allows you to participate in and enjoy the game. The third is to have adequate knowledge of the skills of golf so that you can continue to learn and improve as you play the game.

Rate each of the following aspects of your learning experience:

	Strongly agree	Agree	Disagree	Strongly disagree
1. Overall I learned a great deal in using this book.	_____	_____	_____	_____
2. I improved my golf skills.	_____	_____	_____	_____
3. I enjoy playing golf.	_____	_____	_____	_____
4. I worked hard in following the drill format.	_____	_____	_____	_____
5. I would feel comfortable playing golf with my family or friends.	_____	_____	_____	_____
6. This book is a good resource for helping me learn and practice golf.	_____	_____	_____	_____

PHYSICAL SKILLS OF GOLF

The following is a list of the physical skills and on-course skills used in playing golf. During your practice sessions you may have practiced some or all of them. Please rate yourself in each of the skills you learned.

	Very successful	Fairly successful	Partially successful	Unsuccessful
Setup (consistency)	_____	_____	_____	_____
Grip	_____	_____	_____	_____
Alignment of body	_____	_____	_____	_____
Basic full swing motion				
With irons	_____	_____	_____	_____
With woods	_____	_____	_____	_____
Pitching	_____	_____	_____	_____
Chipping	_____	_____	_____	_____
Putting	_____	_____	_____	_____
Sand				
Explosion shot	_____	_____	_____	_____
Buried lie shot	_____	_____	_____	_____
Uneven lies				
Sidehill	_____	_____	_____	_____
Uphill/downhill	_____	_____	_____	_____

PSYCHOLOGICAL AND MENTAL SKILLS

In order to enjoy the game of golf and to play it successfully, you need several types of mental skills. You need to know the basic terms associated with golf and the rules of the game so that you can play fairly. You need to know and demonstrate the etiquette of golf so that you and your playing partners can enjoy a safe and friendly experience. Also, you must be able to control your thoughts and emotions so that you can confidently and capably demonstrate the skills you practice.

	Understand and can use properly	Can define	Recognize but could not define	Unknown to me
Terminology				
Parts of the golf course	_____	_____	_____	_____
Parts of the golf club	_____	_____	_____	_____
Terms related to scoring (e.g., *birdie, bogey*)	_____	_____	_____	_____
Rules and Penalties				
Lost ball	_____	_____	_____	_____
Out-of-bounds	_____	_____	_____	_____
Water hazards	_____	_____	_____	_____
Hitting the flag	_____	_____	_____	_____
Etiquette				
Order of play	_____	_____	_____	_____
Tending the flag	_____	_____	_____	_____
Playing through	_____	_____	_____	_____

	Always	Sometimes	Never	Unknown to me
Courtesy on the Course				
Replace divots	_____	_____	_____	_____
Rake bunkers	_____	_____	_____	_____
Repair ball marks	_____	_____	_____	_____
Keep carts where they belong	_____	_____	_____	_____
Mental Skills				
Use preshot routine	_____	_____	_____	_____
Use an intermediate target	_____	_____	_____	_____
Use alignment clubs to practice	_____	_____	_____	_____
Avoid negative thoughts and images	_____	_____	_____	_____
Identify the strengths and weaknesses of a hole in order to plan strategy	_____	_____	_____	_____

Now look back at this self-rating inventory. Reread each question and answer carefully. What does it tell you about your golf skills, areas of strength and weakness, and desire to play golf in the future?

Appendix A

Individual Program

INDIVIDUAL COURSE IN _____ GRADE/COURSE SECTION _____

STUDENT'S NAME _____ STUDENT ID # _____

SKILLS/CONCEPTS	TECHNIQUE AND PERFORMANCE OBJECTIVES	WT* ×	POINT PROGRESS** =				FINAL SCORE***
			1	2	3	4	

Note. From "The Role of Expert Knowledge Structures in an Instructional Design Model for Physical Education" by J.N. Vickers, 1983, *Journal of Teaching in Physical Education,* **2**(3), p. 17. Copyright 1983 by Joan N. Vickers. Adapted by permission.

*WT = Weighting of an objective's degree of difficulty.

**PROGRESS = Ongoing success, which may be expressed in terms of (a) accumulated points (1, 2, 3, 4); (b) grades (D, C, B, A); (c) symbols (merit, bronze, silver, gold); (d) unsatisfactory/satisfactory; and others as desired.

***FINAL SCORE equals WT times PROGRESS.

Appendix B

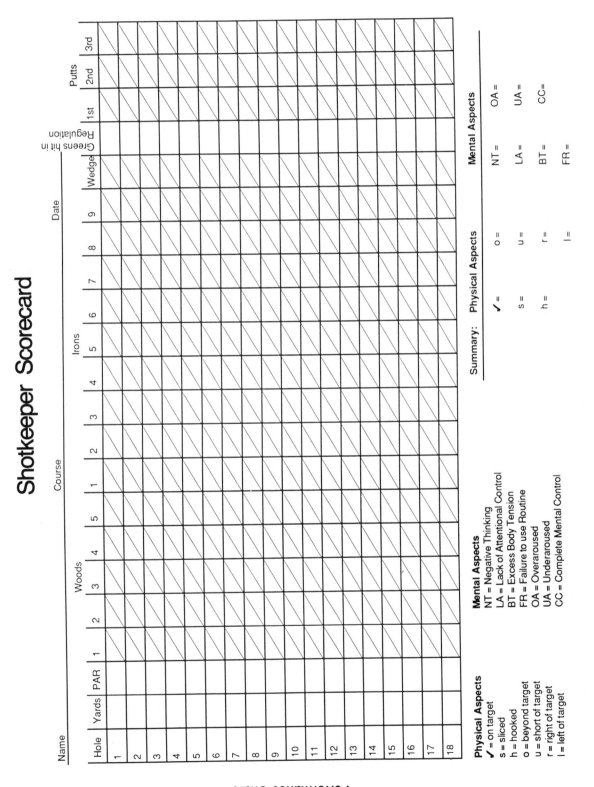

Shotkeeper Scorecard

Name _____ Course _____ Date _____

Performance Chart

Hole	Yards	PAR	Woods 1	2	3	4	5	Irons 1	2	3	4	5	6	7	8	9	Wedge	Greens hit in Regulation	Putts 1st	2nd	3rd
1																					
2																					
3																					
4																					
5																					
6																					
7																					
8																					
9																					
10																					
11																					
12																					
13																					
14																					
15																					
16																					
17																					
18																					

Physical Aspects
✓ = on target
s = sliced
h = hooked
o = beyond target
u = short of target
r = right of target
l = left of target

Mental Aspects
NT = Negative Thinking
LA = Lack of Attentional Control
BT = Excess Body Tension
FR = Failure to use Routine
OA = Overaroused
UA = Underaroused
CC = Complete Mental Control

Summary: **Physical Aspects**

✓ =   o =   s =   u =   h =   r =   l =

Mental Aspects

NT =   OA =   LA =   UA =   BT =   CC=   FR =

211

About the Authors

DeDe Owens, EdD, is the teaching professional at Cog Hill Golf Club in Lemont, Illinois, and a member of *Golf Digest's* instructional staff. A former professional on the Ladies Professional Golf Association tour, she holds the LPGA's Master Teacher ranking, having been cited as their Teacher of the Year in 1978.

In 1986 Dr. Owens received the Joe Graffis Award from the National Golf Foundation for her "outstanding contribution to golf education." This contribution has been made not only through her work as a club professional but also through her teaching at the University of North Carolina, Delta State University, Illinois State University, and the University of Virginia. Dr. Owens is also the author of *Golf for Special Populations* and co-author of *Golf: Better Practice for Better Play*, both published by Leisure Press.

Linda K. Bunker, PhD, is professor of physical education and Associate Dean for Academic and Student Affairs at the University of Virginia. She is a consultant for both the National Golf Foundation and the Ladies Professional Golf Association and is on the advisory boards of the Women's Sport Foundation and the Melpomene Institute, the Minneapolis-based research institute for women in sport.

In the Netherlands Dr. Bunker works as a consultant to the Holland Golf Team, and she has provided golf workshops for PGA professionals from Japan, Holland, and the United States. Widely published, she is the co-author of many other books, including *Mind Mastery for Winning Golf; Mind, Set and Match; Sport Psychology: Maximizing Sport Potential; Parenting Your Superstar;* and *Golf: Better Practice for Better Play*. A former nationally ranked junior tennis player, Dr. Bunker remains an avid tennis player when she is not on the links.